The Fast-Track M

Published in association with PricewaterhouseCoopers

Consultant Editors
John Kind, PricewaterhouseCoopers
David Megginson, Sheffield Business School

THE FAST-TRACK MBA SERIES represents a significantly better and different approach to presenting the essence of a typical business school syllabus in an accessible and lively way.
The usual academic textbook emphasis is put to one side in favour of a practical, highly participative style, drawing the reader to the heart of the real world issues involved.

The series is designed specifically for executives, managers and students worldwide who wish to develop or renew their capabilities. The topics covered give the reader the opportunity to acquire a comprehensive knowledge of business, boosting self-confidence and career prospects. For those who may be attending a business school programme, the series offers a thorough introduction to each subject area – an excellent preparation for more advanced work.
Titles already available in the series are:

- *Accounting and Finance for Managers*, second edition, John Kind
- *Ethics in Organizations*, David J Murray
- *Human Resource Development*, second edition, David Megginson, Jennifer Joy-Matthews and Paul Banfield
- *Human Resource Management*, revised edition, Barry Cushway
- *Innovation and Creativity*, Jonne Ceserani and Peter Greatwood
- *Leadership*, Philip Sadler
- *Macroeconomics*, Keith Wade and Francis Breedon
- *Operations Management*, Donald Waters
- *Organizational Behaviour and Design*, second edition, Barry Cushway and Derek Lodge
- *Strategic Management*, J Craig and R Grant

The Series Editors

John Kind is a director in the human resource consulting practice of PricewaterhouseCoopers and specializes in management training. He has wide experience of designing and presenting business education programmes in various parts of the world for clients such as BAA, Bass, British Petroleum, Burmah-Castrol, DHL and Scottish Amicable Life Assurance Society. He is a visiting lecturer at Henley Management College and holds an MBA from the Manchester Business School and an honours degree in Economics from the University of Lancaster.

David Megginson is a writer and researcher on self-development and the manager as developer. He has written *A Manager's Guide to Coaching, Self-development: A facilitator's guide, Mentoring in Action, Human Resource Development* in the Fast-Track MBA series and *The Line Manager as Developer.* He has also co-authored two major research reports – *Developing the Developers* and *Learning for Success.* He consults and researches in blue chip companies, and public and voluntary organizations. He is chairman of the European Mentoring Centre and an elected Council member of AMED, and has been Associate Head of Sheffield Business School and a National Assessor for the National Training Awards.

PricewaterhouseCoopers is a leading provider of professional services, including accountancy and audit, tax and management consultancy. It is the world's largest professional services practice.

THE *FAST-TRACK* (MBA) SERIES

PROBLEM SOLVING

GRAHAM WILSON

SECOND EDITION

Published in association with

KOGAN
PAGE

First published as *Problem-Solving and Decision-Making*, 1993
Second edition, 2000

Kogan Page Limited
120 Pentonville Road
London
N1 9JN
UK

Kogan Page Limited
163 Central Avenue, Suite 4
Dover
NH 03820
USA

British Library Cataloguing in Publication Data

A CIP record for this book is available from the British Library.

ISBN 0 7494 3032 X

Typeset by Jean Cussons Typesetting, Diss, Norfolk
Printed and bound in Great Britain by Clays Ltd, St Ives plc

Contents

Acknowledgements

Writing a book inevitably places pressure on relatives, friends and colleagues. I should like to thank them all, but especially Gilli, George and Betty, and Donald, for their tolerance and encouragement as I prepared this second edition.

This book reflects the changes that I have been through in recent years, aided and supported by a number of 'teachers'. We all of us have teachers, either formal or informal. When I stopped to reflect on the names of those to include here I realized just how fortunate I have been, and continue to be, in having so many. Sally, Sarah, Karen, Maren, Kendall, Yvonne, Michael and Asha, thank you in particular.

Introduction

Every book has to start somewhere and it seemed relevant to begin this one with a look at how, to my mind at least, some of the assumptions, even myths, about problem solving are changing.

THE CHANGING WORLD OF WORK

The first edition of this book, entitled *Problem Solving and Decision Making*, was written in the wake of the so-called 'Total Quality' revolution. Throughout the 1980s, there had been a call for managers to change their approach to employees. This shift appeared in many different guises but the theme was the same. Companies involved with Japanese organizations were exposed to their manufacturing methods, which took employee involvement to new levels. Tom Peters was calling for a dramatic revolution in managerial style to become one that took a real interest in people and their development in the name of improved service. The US trade union movement, followed by the US government, was calling for improvements in the 'quality of work-life'. In the United Kingdom, the DTI had encouraged improvements in quality through increased control and systematization, and yet running counter to this was a growth in the use of teams initially for problem solving and then for overall management. Slowly we saw more and more training courses for 'facilitation' skills.

Against this backdrop of managers learning to relax and lead more by listening than telling and workforce members being given unprecedented responsibility and control over their own work, was a major recession. The warning signs were first experienced in the construction industry, before the economic collapse hit manufacturing, the business services and then consumer services sectors. For at least five years, people ceased to feel secure in their jobs. Once and for all the concept of lifetime employment was laid to rest. As with any event, there will have been a few people who managed to escape but this was by far the exception. Organizations – household names – struggled to survive. They laid off workers, axed perks and fringe benefits, sold off unwanted assets (if they could), restructured, re-engineered, and refinanced. Eventually some pulled through; others did not. If anyone has any doubt about the severity of the economic downturn let them drive through some of the suburbs of any major city in the United Kingdom and they will see the grey belt of 'prime' factory building land. They'll see huge industrial premises built in the 1970s and 1980s lying derelict, windows smashed, blinds still flapping, security patrol notices hanging by a single cable tied to the fence.

Throughout the few years before the recession, during it, and then just afterwards, whole 'industries' were broken down into parts, reassembled and now work in different ways. The majority of us couldn't have imagined such a transition. Take the rail industry, for example, where the single major nationalized body has been broken down into a myriad of components each in the private sector. Or the health service that no longer offers some of the services that our parents and grandparents took for granted.

Ten years ago, you would probably never have shopped in an out-of-town supermarket; you would have only just begun to hear of e-mail but certainly not the Internet. You probably knew of cellular telephones but were frightened to buy one because there were too many sharks out there selling them. Of course there are always critics and advocates of these kinds of changes and I have no interest in being judgmental. The point is that change really has happened and some of us have been affected by it less in our work than in our out-of-work hours.

Activity I.1

It might be worth your while spending a few minutes reflecting for your-self on the extent to which your own workplace has changed in the last 10 years. You might have still been at school or university, so consider how they have changed in that time too.

THE CHANGING WORLD OF GRAHAM WILSON

Sometimes I feel disheartened when I hear someone going on about their discovery of some new, radical approach to X, Y or Z. So often it seems that there is nothing new or radical. I'm getting old, of course. Only last week I was offered the 'latest insights into radical management thinking' on a three-day facilitation skills training course. We've been running programmes of this kind for over a decade so it was bound to attract my attention. Was there anything different? No, only the names of the presenters. But there is a difference. Ten years ago, facilitation skills were considered 'fringe'; they were touchy-feely stuff or as a colleague then said, 'It's just some kind of synchronized hand waving.' Today, if a manager isn't skilled at facilitation then they have a real problem. My own practice often has senior managers referred to it because their 'behaviour' (something they were selected for and subsequently have honed over 15 or more years) is no longer considered acceptable to the company.

Ten years ago, subjects that would have been considered so way off-beam that their advocates were thought to have been from another planet are still fringe; but they have a manyfold increase in their supporters. For example, if you work in London for an office-based company, there is a good chance that your rooms will have been Feng Shui'd and perhaps visited by a crystal healer. Let's be honest, even today that will raise an eyebrow or two in a lot of quarters but 10 years ago you'd have been lucky to find a smoke-free room!

So where have I been over the last few years and how has that changed my approach to problem solving?

The old approach: how to solve problems

Around the time that the first edition was appearing, I began to feel uncomfortable about some of the lessons that I had learnt during my managerial career. I was considered part of the 'new guard' working in the area of OD (organization development) concerned with self-directed work groups as an outcome to business process re-engineering activities. I taught team-based problem solving as part of this and much of the first edition was based on this work. In that book, we looked at the dynamics of teams and how they affected people 'doing' problem solving. Then I began to work with a number of clients (and in one consultancy organization) where I could see that it didn't matter what they did systematically and using the best techniques, the problems were always there. The 'problems' were the individuals, what they brought with them to the group, and the dynamics between them. It didn't matter how logical the argument that was presented, how well it was put, or how convincing the evidence, the people would accept all that but still had problems.

It began to dawn on me, and I feel rather foolish saying it this way but I know there are many more like me, that the lessons I had learnt from work were at best faulty and at worst downright counterproductive. What is the point in bludgeoning people, no matter how subtly, with brainstorming, Pareto charts and fancy surveys, into tackling some set of symptoms regarding their production process or whatever, if the real problem is still not being spoken about let alone dealt with?

So I went into my next meeting, a particularly sticky one with a managing director. I tried so hard to find out what his REAL issues were, but each time I thought I'd seen through his 'agenda' to something deeper and more important he poured scorn on the idea and reverted back to his demands for greater sales volume. I decided to go back to school; to enrol for a basic counselling course in the hope that if my skills were improved I'd be able to 'tackle' people like this MD better. That was the starting point of a journey that is still going on. Through my training in counselling and psychotherapy, I have begun to uncover for myself some of the symptoms and a few of the reasons why these problems arise, what happens and how to work with them.

The new approach: focus on what the problems are

In preparing the first edition, I spent a lot of time reviewing other problem solving books. I found a startling lack of variety. What most had was a structured approach to dealing with an explicit symptom, eg 'We know we can market on the Internet, but what can we do about it?' This usually calls for some insight into the possible approaches. Then we look at ways of addressing this – often by focusing on the obstacles that are the most significant and finding ways of counteracting them. In my book I tried to put this into a context of the new organization, one where problems were tackled by teams, initially on an *ad hoc* basis but increasingly as part of their normal day-to-day work. This approach was unique then and is still largely so today. While companies are no longer clamouring for team-based structures, the power of involvement remains very strong and so the emphasis on a team-based solution remains in this edition. You'll find nothing missing in that sense, and I remain convinced that there have been no new tomes that add much to this area.

So what is new in this book? Well, we are going to explore two new aspects of problems that are certainly as widespread in organizations if not more so than the more obvious explicit symptom and its solution. We are going to look at problems that arise within and between *large* groups and at those that involve *single* individuals. These problems usually involve conflict, what some would describe as nasty, painful, and sometimes violent, conflict.

Activity I.2

You've decided to read a book on problem solving. Before we go on, I wonder if you'd like to try putting a pen to paper and asking yourself what the 'problems' are that you would like to tackle? It might help you get more out of the book and focus your mind anyway. You might like to choose to do this with a bullet list or you could try writing a short story that you could even illustrate.

JUST HOW SERIOUS IS 'PROBLEM SOLVING' AS A SUBJECT?

Many people used to think, and some still do, of problem solving as a kind of carpetbag of tools. When a problem occurs, the GP will reach for the pad, write out a prescription for some pills or a potion, and before you can say 'Take these twice a day', the problem has gone. We all know that this isn't true.

Managers, as opposed to the general public, often describe 'problem solving' as a kind of fire fighting. I remember a few years ago running one of my first courses in problem solving. The Chief Executive of the oil company who had commissioned the course insisted on attending for a 'pep' talk in the evening of the first day. We sat next to one another at dinner and he explained to me that his rapid rise through the company was because he had become known as an excellent problem solver. I was delighted until he explained that, of course, no one realized that he had started most of the fires himself! Too often, certain managers will be lambasted for spending too much time fire fighting and not enough time dealing with strategy. If that isn't their particular failing then they'll be told that their problem-solving ability (or inability really) is what is holding them back from promotion.

If this sounds cynical then perhaps I am just getting a little jaded. Fortunately, in the late 1970s the concept of continuous improvement took off and added respectability to the idea of tackling problems in a structured way. When continuous improvement was consumed by total quality, the whole subject became a strategic issue. By the early 1990s it was being recognized that in order to survive, organizations needed an injection of innovation and the focus of problem solving changed again – this time to both innovation rather than retrospective fixing and from a strategic choice to a survival need.

Today, I believe, problem solving is entering new territory. The first dimension is to explore ways of solving problems in an unstructured manner rather than purely in a linear analytical way. The second is to accept openly that many problems have their roots in the relationships between people – individually, in pairs, collectively in groups or *en masse.* In this book you'll find these new dimensions being explored probably for the first time in a mainstream management text.

WHERE PROBLEMS OCCUR AND WHY

If you ask people at work what sort of problems they encounter on a day-to-day basis, they will usually mention four themes:

1. Time management – getting everything they 'need' to do done in the time they have.
2. Excessive paperwork and information – something that the information technology age seems to have contributed to rather than solved.
3. 'Selling' their ideas to other people – no longer being able to rely on positions of power to influence.
4. Difficulties in relationships with colleagues.

In the following chapters there's plenty of material to help you explore these and other problems. Hopefully too, you'll find some things that you didn't expect to find. This is because we are slowly accepting that 'problems' have their origins in far wider areas than just the confines of a production line or a telephone call centre. Before we go much further, I'd like to suggest a few minutes reflection by yourself. The following exercise tries to help this. Through the book you'll find little exercises like this, they are intended to help and I hope that you'll give them the time they deserve.

Activity I.3

Find somewhere reasonably quiet and don't start doing something else. This will only take a few minutes but it is worth the effort if you are really going to benefit from this book.

On a single sheet of A4 paper, somewhere near the middle put the word 'problems'. Now think back over the last week. Try to remember what you were doing and then ask yourself why. Each time that you realize that you were there because of a problem, or while you were there a problem arose, or someone came to you with a problem, jot a couple of words anywhere on the paper to sum up the situation.

Don't restrict yourself to work and work-related problems, what about home, your partner, your children, your community, your car, and so on? What were you doing last weekend? How much of that time was sorting out problems? Why is it that your daughter only remembered to tell you about the gym competition on Friday evening after you'd already planned who was going to do the weekend shopping? Another problem to be solved.

After a little while of doing this, as your mind begins to dry up, look at the paper and see if there are any patterns. Are the problems mainly ones of logistics, relationships, products, or whatever?

Use this paper record as a bookmark with this book. It'll help remind you of the focus you should have as you read it, whether you do so from cover-to-cover or by dipping in.

ARE ALL PROBLEMS BAD?

I hope that this isn't the only strange question that you'll encounter in this book. Think about it for a few moments though. Are *all* problems bad? Some 'problems' are simply patterns that happen in our lives and there's little that we can do about them except stop worrying! To be fair they may still be bad, but the thing that causes us the discomfort is not the problem but the worrying. As Dale Carnegie (1948) puts it, 'Stop worrying and start living!' Don't keep beating yourself (and others) up for something that is a fact of life. You have to take a responsible approach to this but it is a fundamental start to tackling problems in the first place and is often the difference between creativity and problem solving.

Another, perhaps more contentious question is whether the 'problem' is actually enjoyable! Go on, do you get a kick out of it? I had a neighbour recently who was employed by an airline as a roving 'customer service' manager. Having been in operations, his job was now to go out to see major corporate clients and resolve their 'problems'. He found the whole idea depressing. His 'buzz' was out of being in the hub of operations. He felt that travelling by car was tedious. He found that many of the 'problems' were excuses for not paying bills. He also found that the clients he was dealing with were often gloomy, bored, unexcited, and generally not very inspiring to deal with. In fact, their complaining was probably their way of putting some interest into their work! We spent an hour or so in conversation, doing what neurolinguistic programming (NLP) practitioners would call re-framing. Out of that he saw that he could radically transform these people's lives, put a little bit of excitement and fun back in and direct their energy in a much more constructive way. How? He still went around and saw them, and listened, and did what he could to 'fix' the immediate concern. Then he would add, as a parting shot, 'I don't know if you'd be interested, but next Thursday afternoon, I'm taking a few people on a tour "behind the scenes" at the airport. If you'd like to come along you'd be welcome.' He fixed up a monthly tour, and hosted a couple of dozen people each time. Even customers who had been perpetual complainers, stopped almost overnight!

To use that awful cliché, some problems really are opportunities!

DO 'STRUCTURED' APPROACHES REALLY WORK?

You are going to find this book a hybrid. Its origin is in a first edition that followed the pattern of problem-solving books by presenting a structured approach, a linear model, for tackling problems systematically. As I've said elsewhere, my own thinking has changed and I no longer see this as the only means of solving problems. The reason I feel this way is that my definition of 'problems' has broadened. There were always unstructured approaches around but they weren't often referred to because people didn't see the problems they addressed as 'business' ones. I no longer think that this is the case. Increasingly people in organizations are tackling broader issues than directly work-related ones. It is in these circumstances that the 'structured approach' no longer really works.

Let me give just two examples. I recently ran some coaching workshops for a large petrochemical company. The 'problems' they had were symptomatic of an under-investment in management development among the longer-serving (you might say 'senior') staff. The problems revolved around their attitudes to each other and especially to the people whose work they were expected to manage. The company had previously taken a structured approach and organized workshops on leadership and diversity to raise these issues and address them. They failed miserably because the managers scorned the organizers, the tutors, the material and the facilities of the place where the workshops were being run. Their attitudes were again the problem. We took a different approach. In our sessions, we simply let them talk. They talked about their lives, their responsibilities, their frustrations, the things they saw as unfair in their work and outside, the irritations they had to deal with, their ambitions and how these had evolved since they were young. We never once discussed their attitudes, or the symptoms of them at work. However, over quite a short period of time, in fact after three or four sessions in most cases, the local HR representative reported a significant shift in their relationships with other staff. The annual employee attitude survey endorsed this trend. They were becoming more tolerant of their own 'failings' as they saw them, and so becoming more tolerant of others.

The second example is of Motorola. They have a programme in place to provide further training for those teachers working with young children in South America. South America is their largest market growth opportunity for the next few years. Why teach teachers? For several reasons, but three in particular. Let's face it – it's good PR for a company to be seen to be altruistic in a market where political decisions are going to be taken that will enable or inhibit your opportunity for growth. Then there's the level of illiteracy, which is such that they know they'll have a job recruiting local people to operate their factories. And the same level of illiteracy is going to stop people buying the company's mobile phones and using them because of the difficulty of reading the instructions. Put that way, the 'solution' is a natural answer that could easily have been arrived at through a structured approach. I'm tempted to say, 'Come on – get real!' Could you conceivably have sold such an idea to your peers and shareholders?

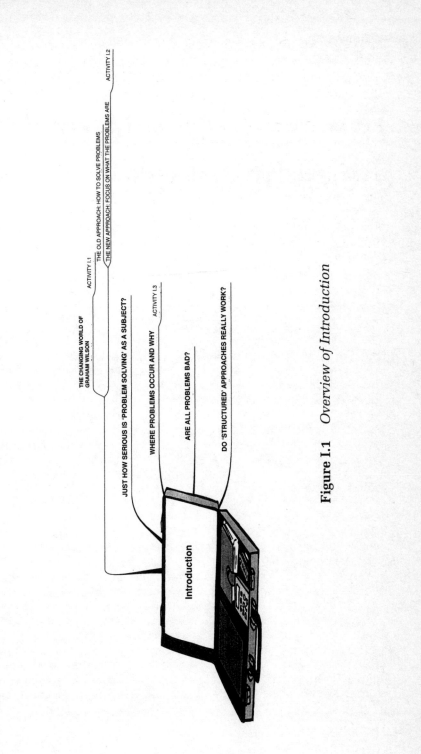

THE CHANGING WORLD OF
GRAHAM WILSON

ACTIVITY I.1

THE OLD APPROACH: HOW TO SOLVE PROBLEMS
THE NEW APPROACH: FOCUS ON WHAT THE PROBLEMS ARE

ACTIVITY I.2

JUST HOW SERIOUS IS 'PROBLEM SOLVING' AS A SUBJECT?

ACTIVITY I.3

WHERE PROBLEMS OCCUR AND WHY

ARE ALL PROBLEMS BAD?

DO 'STRUCTURED' APPROACHES REALLY WORK?

Introduction

Figure I.1 *Overview of Introduction*

CHAPTER I

The right climate and the right culture

CASE STUDY 1.1

One November evening a few years ago, Elizabeth Mauras was on duty at the room service desk of the Bethesda Marriott Hotel in downtown Maryland. Early in the evening she received a call from a female guest on business in the town. The guest had checked in and had decided to order from room service rather than visit the restaurant. Mauras took the order and began processing it. A few minutes – and several calls – later, the guest rang again, this time to cancel her order. There can be many reasons for guests cancelling orders and it is not an unusual occurrence. But in this particular case something worried Elizabeth Mauras.

The Marriott organization is constantly trying to achieve high levels of customer service through its employees. At the time the emphasis was on encouraging the staff to find innovative solutions to guests' problems, to be highly responsive, taking authority and responsibility and generally being very people-focused.

As a result of her training, not only was Elizabeth Mauras concerned about the guest's cancellation from a commercial perspective, but she also suspected that the reason for it might be significant. She asked the *maître d'hôtel* to cover for her while she went to the guest's room. Knocking on the door, she introduced herself and explained quickly why she was there, and then listened to the customer. It transpired that the guest, having ordered her food from room service, rang home – only to discover that her mother had been taken seriously ill, was in hospital and wasn't expected to survive the night. She had rung the airport to find out whether there was time for her to catch the last flight home, only to realize that it would not be possible for her to get to the airport in time.

The guest was understandably distressed. It had been Mauras's sensitive ears and quick perception that had enabled her to recognize the distress in the customer's voice when she had cancelled the room service order. Mauras rang the airport, explained the situation and asked the airline to hold the flight at the expense of the Marriott organization, summoned the bellboy to help the guest with her bags, and had the doorman hold a cab. As a result of Mauras's bold actions, the guest was able to make the flight and was at her mother's bedside that night when she passed away.

This is rather a sad anecdote with which to begin a book on problem solving, but I believe it sets the context perfectly. For people in many organizations such bold action would have been effectively suicidal. For a 'mere' room service operator to commit the organization to several hundreds of thousands of pounds worth of liability, to behave so decisively after perceiving the customer's distress, is a long way removed from our day-to-day reality. That the organization should have developed an employee who was capable of such actions, and created an environment in which she was able to do this, is quite remarkable; that they then went on to advertise such behaviour to the rest of their employees is not just remarkable, to many proprietors of businesses it would seem downright naïve.

Yet organizations are changing. It is now a cliché to say that 'change is the only constant'.[1] For decades we have been subjected to change – technological, legislative, financial, in our working practices, in our products, in our market-places. Change is certainly all around us.

HOW HAS YOUR ORGANIZATION CHANGED?

Groups

In recent years, organizations have moved away from using individuals taking actions in isolation and towards working more and more in groups or teams. Accompanying this trend towards group working has been far greater devolution of authority and responsibility. Groups now take virtually any decision in an organization: ordering materials and supplies, scheduling work, conducting maintenance, testing product quality, hiring and firing, and so on.

Leadership

Accompanying the shift of power to groups, the role of the manager has also changed. Few perhaps would admit to it but, in the past, the role of the manager has often been to police, to control, acting almost as a self-appointed representative of justice in the organization. Of course, even today, there are managers who would be amazed at the suggestion that employees should monitor their own holiday allowances, should be responsible for scheduling their own work, for discipline, for safety, and so on! In many organizations the manager has been the linchpin of information and would be shocked to hear that the weekly or monthly team meeting is going to be chaired by a rotating panel of members. As groups acquire more sophisticated tools and techniques, it is not unusual for them to carry out an analysis of members' strengths and weaknesses. Often one person will be found to have particular skills at chairing meetings and he or she will be chosen to carry out this role instead of the manager. The person chairing the meeting is acting as a member of the team and not deriving any power from the role.

As managers have handed over authority and responsibility, they have taken on a further responsibility themselves for the development of their staff. Of course, managers who have been particularly authoritarian are likely to find this transition difficult. But for many it is a role that they have always wanted, but have never had time for before.

The role of the leader has also changed, I would suggest. In the past, studies of leaders have shown them to have quite specific aspects to their personalities. These have included many less desirable facets too. Today, leaders are becoming more aware of themselves and what drives them. They are looking at their past and how it has shaped their personalities and at how they want to (and whether they should want to) shape the lives of others. There is a revolution taking place today around leadership and the qualities that make a leader.

Culture

It has been the vogue for many years now to try to consciously change the culture of organizations. We discuss this in more detail in a subsequent chapter, but for the moment it is worth thinking about some of the involuntary changes that have happened.

Problem solving in organizations that are autonomous is going to be different from problem solving in those that are tightly controlled subsidiaries. It is going to be different if you are in the parent company and are trying to implement change in a subsidiary. Following mergers, resolving problems can be complex and drawn-out, whereas before, decisions could be taken easily and implemented quickly. In each case finding the solution to a problem may be the easy part – it is the implementation of it that is tough.

Speed

It has been said that today is the era of speed. The technology that we use enables us to transmit information and documents instantaneously. Just-in-time, achieved through efficient business processes, was a management concept that had its heyday in the late 1980s but it is still a sensible goal for organizations to aspire to unless they seek to be less efficient for social reasons (see 'tradition', below).

Delivery overnight is the norm and some companies, like the Viking Direct stationery company, are challenging this by delivering the same day in many principal cities. Despite this, there are still some companies that don't recognize the importance of timely delivery and still insist on four-week lead times on orders. One Mumbai-based computer peripherals manufacturer takes less than that to deliver stocks of newly designed inkjet printers from the Indian factory where they are produced to the distribution point of a major US computer manufacturer. It seems pretty poor that I can order a book from an Internet bookseller (of all people) and still have to wait up to four weeks for it to be delivered!

Many problem-solving activities focus on how to make things more efficient or propose technology-based solutions. Yet often the things that slow us down are not technology-based or inefficient processes. Why does it take companies 60 or more days to pay an invoice that was due the day it was presented? There are human decisions – individual or policy-led – at play here, not machine or process problems.

It is a constant source of amazement to me how long it takes organizations to recognize individuals who have made a special effort and done something really good for them. Often it has to wait until the next annual performance review and even then it might be missed!

The other evening, a friend, David Bell, showed me the Military Medal and Bar that were awarded to his grandfather during the First World War. Having already been awarded the Military Medal, the highest military honour that could be awarded to non-commissioned officers in the United Kingdom, Lance Corporal Bell went out into no-man's land, under enemy artillery fire, traced, found the breaks in and repaired three telephone lines and returned safely. His actions kept his command post in contact with the troops for nearly a day and a half. This will almost certainly have contributed to the success of their part of the battle at Ypres and probably saved many lives. How long did it take the powers that be to award him the Bar to his medal? Fourteen days. It may have seemed a lifetime under those conditions, but it shames most management teams today.

Technology

It barely seems possible that the PC has only been with us 25 years or so. This isn't the place to applaud the escalating power of microprocessor technology, but it is worth reflecting on areas that haven't been affected by the power of the computer and asking why.

There are still booming sectors of the economy that depend on good old-fashioned sweat to make things happen. Equally there are areas of the world that have still to get a power supply to connect a PC to. And before they get that their priority is water and sanitation. Why do I make this point? Because it is all too easy for us to slip into a must-have mentality when we tackle problems in our organization. Throwing technology at an issue may help, but it may exacerbate the problem and it is often worth looking at low-tech solutions first.

The workplace

While organizations with a large office or plant can organize themselves in groups, there are a growing number of companies offering staff the opportunity to work from home. At first this was largely restricted to non-managerial people, but increasingly it applies to all staff. Not only does this make the problem of involvement in day-to-day improvement initiatives a tough one, but it also makes it harder to sell in solutions. It's necessary to make major efforts to keep these staff involved and engaged in the process of change.

But home working isn't the only change that has happened in the workplace. The growth of the leisure industry means that more and more people no longer wear suits and work in offices. A more relaxed style and more relaxed environment call for different approaches to management and leadership. Traditional means of exerting power, bigger cars, more expensive clothes and more of them, larger offices and being seen to go out 'on business' are no longer necessary, and no longer impress. With the loss of power of this kind, individuals whose authority would never be challenged are now open to question by almost anyone. Again, this all has an effect on leadership and management.

Tradition

Change doesn't just affect tangibles like technology. It also affects intangibles like our motives and aspirations for doing things. I remember a conversation with the MD of a large company who was describing self-directed work groups as an impossibility in the United Kingdom along with employee buy-outs. He assured me that 'workers' couldn't own and run businesses. He obviously hadn't heard of the John Lewis Partnership, which has done just that for a century!

There are many such 'assumptions', I prefer to call them 'traditions', about the way in which things should (and here it becomes 'must') be run. These are rich fodder for the problem-solving group. Question everything, don't allow yourselves to be undermined by such dogma. For example, can an organization succeed commercially while paying significantly more to its manufacturers than its competitors do? Body Shop would say so. Should organizations always seek to maximize the return to their investors through profit? Not if they are a co-operative seeking to employ larger numbers of people. Examples of tradition breaking abound. It simply takes a few brave souls in the organization to challenge accepted wisdom.

Activity 1.1

Do a little research for yourself. Try to draw up a short history of your organization. Document the key steps in its evolution from its beginnings. See how change has happened and where and when. Involve someone from purchasing who can tell you about significant purchases, new equipment, computers, and so on. Interview the HR director and see if you can tie down significant changes in employee numbers and locations. And so on. Who knows, you might even end up with a publishable story. One organization, Atlantic Richfield (ARCO), has produced its history as a mural on display in the front lobby of its offices.

ORGANIZING FOR INNOVATION

If our goal is to improve the innovativeness of the organization as a whole or of a part of it, rather than tackling specific problems, then there are some things that we can do to maximize our chances.

Small teams

Whether your organization has a history of working in teams or not, the best way to introduce innovation rapidly is to do so. Ideally, reorganize your area completely. If that is too much of a risk, then at least create a small team as a pilot, monitor their success and then cascade the approach.

Mixed backgrounds

When forming teams, make sure that they don't consist of the same type of people. Don't establish new functions, think quickly and laterally of the types of skills that might be needed to find solutions to a particular problem, then select a few people representing each of those skills to make up the team.

If you want to be more systematic about the selection process, then assemble a team using Belbin's team roles (see also Chapter 4) as a guide.[2] You probably need a Chairperson – not someone who has been selected because of their position, but someone who is genuinely good at marshalling the ideas and contributions of others; in many cases, the less that the Chairperson knows about the subject the better!

The team can work on new ideas or build on existing ones. For this process Belbin and his team identified two common team roles – the Plant, who has a talent for introducing new ideas, and the Shaper, who moulds other people's suggestions or existing approaches. If the solution is likely to involve outside agencies, either providing information, physical resources or staff, then a Resource Investigator is a useful contributor to the team. This kind of person is skilled at finding (and tapping) external resources.

A team with a Chairperson, a Plant or Shaper and a Resource Investigator would probably produce a good attempt at a preliminary solution. Unfortunately they might not be quite so good at taking this through to conclusion. The fourth member therefore needs to be a Completer–Finisher. This individual will make sure that the others consider how the ideas can be implemented in practice and that the problem is resolved speedily.

Of course, there may be other people in the team, although they should still be chosen for a purpose. Any of my former colleagues from one company will recognize a team that consisted almost entirely of Shapers. Everyone had the best idea, everyone began and then never finished it, everyone resented the others for having had the same idea and so on!

What we have said implies that someone is making a choice of the team (and certainly of the leader) as to who should be included. Unless you are the team leader it is important for you to think through the implications of choosing on their behalf. If the choice of problem(s) to tackle lies with more senior managers then it is not unusual for these managers to also suggest who should take part. On the other hand, people working on a particular problem that they have chosen for themselves will expect to have been self-selected. We often find the best compromise is for the team leader to work with a facilitator and apply the Belbin team roles approach to potential members. This allows the leader to retain full responsibility, teaches them some new skills, and introduces some objectivity into a potentially very subjective area.

Short timescales

If you want the team to produce quick results they have to know what is expected of them and they need to have the freedom to achieve it. It is pointless saying that you want a result in three weeks if the team only has the opportunity to meet once in that time. Almost all problems involve some discussion, followed by some data gathering, followed by further discussion.

Targets often do need to be set, but they must not become tablets of stone. If they do, the people within the team who are highly task orientated will start to take over and as a result the solution will probably not work in practice.

It is usual to give a suggested timescale as a guide and let the team make the final decision. A common scenario is for a management team to commission a group to work on something, brief them, and then complain because the group has not done what they were asked to a timescale that they had not been informed of. The easiest way to overcome this is to impose a short timescale, but this may involve too much control and not enough delegation. Within the timescale set the team must be given complete authority to work as it sees fit, and the management team must recognize that it can remain involved without taking over.

Complete authority

It goes without saying that unless you are an exception, the team will be working within realistic frameworks. Let's face it, the Manhattan project, which pulled together nuclear scientists from around the world to develop the atomic bomb in a very short space of time, is not happening every day of the week. Although groups should be working on projects of significance (if they're not, what *are* they doing?) they are likely to be constrained to some extent.

Some textbooks used to suggest (and the contemporary materials based on them still do) that managers should only delegate to the point of decision-making. The argument was that then the team could not cause problems by making too ambitious a commitment. Many organizations today are recognizing that the people in teams know as much as, if not more than, their immediate superiors about the problems that they are tackling. Certainly, the higher up the hierarchy people are, the less they will know about detailed, day-to-day issues.

Teams regulate themselves. They are unlikely to be 'out of control' unless the problem that they are dealing with is beyond their experience. If it is, then the original choice of leader and team members was wrong. Although it is a difficult stance to adopt, especially at first, if you want a team to develop genuinely innovative solutions then you have to give its members the authority that they need.

There are different ways of doing this. We often hear people describe one of the pitfalls of teams as finding themselves confronted by other people in the organization. These people were enforcing the 'rules' as they saw them. The solutions vary – most either issue a general edict that the teams will be given every assistance or they appoint a senior manager as a mentor/champion. If they have been trying to achieve a change in culture through the teams, then they haven't made a thorough enough job of the stages for successful change that are described in Chapter 13. Issuing edicts can work, as can telling the team to work around the problem, but appointing champions is almost always self-defeating as the team begins to see the champion as someone who they have to consult before doing anything – indeed, quite a few champions like this too!

There's no getting away from it that the only reasonable solution is to give teams complete authority. Most barriers that confront teams fall into one of two groups: finance or people. To deal with financial problems the team leader needs to be made aware that the project has a budget but that it is open-ended. The team members should only incur personal expenses in line with normal business practice – if they think that this means hiring helicopters to travel to and from meetings, then you need to ask yourself where they got this idea from! Expenditure on prototypes and so on needs to be justified, as any other business investment would, to the organization's auditors, but if the team feels that it can justify the expense then it should be allowed to proceed.

One suggestion for dealing with people who have a problem with the team's activities is to ask the team leader to refer those people to you, the manager. If you are bombarded with referrals then you need to look at the culture of the organization to identify the root cause of the problem. If people are referred to you then check why the team felt it had to do this and treat it as a learning opportunity for its members but recognize that it is also an opportunity for you to keep in touch with the team's progress without interfering. If no one is referred to you, ask yourself whether you were available – if you weren't, reconsider your role.

Be involved but don't take over

If teams tackling problems are a rare event in your organization, the members will not feel entirely at ease with the way in which they are being watched over. You need to do enough to relax them without stepping in and taking control.

There are three approaches to this: have them report to you; use a network of spies or informants; or take the mountain to Mohammed. If the team feels that it has to report to you, whether through the team leader or a champion, it will be constrained by what it thinks you will consider acceptable limits. If you use a network of spies, then as soon as this comes to light all your credibility will be lost. The solution that is by far the simplest, the most fun and the most effective is for you to visit them. Leave the motorcade behind and don't take a crowd with you – simply drop in. If the timescales that you have suggested are short you will only need to do this a couple of times. Ask the team leader to give you a schedule of the team's meetings and say that you will call in if you can to see if there is anything that the team needs.

CASE STUDY 1.2

A team working on revising a company's paperwork and administrative systems was briefed and told to report back within six weeks. It was asked to give the chief executive a copy of its schedule and told that if he could he would call in to see if they needed any help. The business had around 1,200 employees on 12 main sites. The team met around the country and comprised a range of employees from frontline operators to middle managers.

At the team's third meeting, at one of the more remote locations, the members settled down to a day of business. After about 10 minutes there was a knock on the door and the chief executive put his head round the door. Not entering properly he said, 'I had a spare morning and wondered if you'd mind me sitting in?'

It would have taken a brave person to refuse. He took up a position outside the circle of the group, out of the line of sight of the leader and the facilitator, and sat quietly throughout, deflecting any statements that were unconsciously directed towards him on to the leader. Shortly before lunchtime he offered to arrange some extra resources that they had been talking about, then repeated that they had only to ask if they needed anything, thanked them for letting him join in and left the room.

Was he daft? Did he have nothing better to do? Was he interfering? No – he was involved but he was not taking over.

Demonstrate obsession and add drama

The chief executive in the above example had travelled to the site the previous evening and taken the site manager out to supper – in the process, creating a loyal supporter. His car was waiting for him when he left the meeting. Before it had left the site gates he had arranged for the promised resources to be delivered and they were waiting for the team members when they returned from lunch in the canteen. They were left in no doubt that the chief executive was serious, that their project was serious, and that *they* were in charge.

Most organization development specialists agree that demonstrating obsession produces dramatic results. Despite this, most senior managers are reluctant to step outside their comfort zones and try it out. Even the relatively simple task of 'walking the job' or 'managing by wandering around', which was so popular as a panacea a few years ago (and which still works!), is not often carried out by managers.

From time to time in my consultancy work, I'll be confronted with a management team that appears to be remote from the workforce. We use a simple exercise to understand some of the constraints and set more demanding expectations. They are each given a matrix of the kind shown in Figure 1.1 and are asked to complete it. Then we share the results and discuss them. Figure 1.2 shows the outcome of a typical consensus after this discussion.

	0–250 employees	250–1000 employees	1000+ employees
1 site			
2–5 sites			
6–20 sites			
20+ sites and international			

Figure 1.1   *Frequency of shopfloor contact – blank for use in discussions*

	0–250 employees	250–1000 employees	1000+ employees
1 site	Daily	3–4 times each week	2–3 times each week
2–5 sites	2–3 times each week	Weekly	Weekly/ Fortnightly
6–20 sites	Weekly	Weekly/ Fortnightly	Fortnightly
20+ sites and international	Fortnightly	Every three weeks	Monthly

Figure 1.2   *Frequency of shopfloor contact – typical consensus*

Do away with perks

As an example of demonstrating commitment, the story of a Xerox plant manager, Renn Zaphiropoulos, is hard to beat. Arriving for the first time at the plant on a Monday morning, he walked into his secretary's office and asked for the maintenance engineer to be sent to him. When the engineer had gone, Zaphiropoulos began a series of telephone calls. Later in the morning, to the amazement of his staff, he went down to the car park, put on a factory overall and, using the materials supplied by the maintenance engineer, began painting out the 'Reserved' spaces in the car park. The television reporters that had assembled in response to his telephone calls captured the event.

Benefits such as reserved parking spaces reinforce hierarchies, hierarchies promote positional power, and positional power cramps innovation. Perks fall on either side of the line. They are either positive perks or negative ones. Positive perks either need to be made available to all or done away with. Negative perks need to be done away with and the system needs to be changed to prevent them occurring again. Abolishing such divisive benefits can save money – work out the cost of operating two canteens or two different timekeeping systems, for example.

It can cost very little to make other benefits available to all and this can shatter 'us/them' divides. One petroleum company allowed 'professionals' to travel first class but other grades had to travel second class. If mixed groups were travelling to the same meeting then they had to sit apart. This was not only humiliating, it caused everyone embarrassment and was constantly circumvented by the people involved. The cost of allowing everyone to travel first class was only a few thousand pounds a year.

The availability of certain kinds of support is another good example. The same company would allow 'professionals' to take extended leave in the form of a kind of sabbatical every five years. Not many took advantage of this, but 'non-professionals' were not even allowed to apply. The company would also pay for day release training for graduates (ie professionals in their terms) but not help with Open University studies (almost always undertaken by 'non-professionals'). None of these schemes – even though they were intended to motivate – helped morale. Most hindered collaboration and prevented contributions from those that mattered most – the people who knew the answers!

Involve customers

For many years management scientists have tried to establish a causal relationship between consumer satisfaction and corporate performance. Unfortunately, their efforts have not been entirely successful. There is, however, a good deal of anecdotal evidence of the link.

When trying to boost creativity within an organization the focus may be on various areas: some companies want to see more realistic administrative systems, some better production and service delivery, and some better products and services. The first two of these could be tackled in isolation, without considering outside influences. Probably the simplest way to generate new ideas on the third is to involve customers. It is surprising how many organizations that claim to have embarked on some form of organization development process three, four or even five years ago have never involved their customers.

People in many organizations assume that they know better than their customers. Yet, in practice, every customer has something to say that ought to be listened to. In the range of customers that an organization deals with there is a continuum from 'never again' to 'devoted users'. This continuum can be subdivided as shown in Figure 1.3. Organizations wanting to promote innovation need to make sure that they consult customers in all these groups. The continuum mainly considers customers outside the organization. The concept of the internal customer is a familiar one today. If your part of the organization has nothing to do with external customers (and watch out because your days may be numbered!), my experience is that internal customers have just as much to contribute as external ones, but they are usually much more reluctant to offer it.

It is worth reviewing who your customers are. What mechanisms do you have to obtain feedback from them? And how is this information communicated throughout your organization?

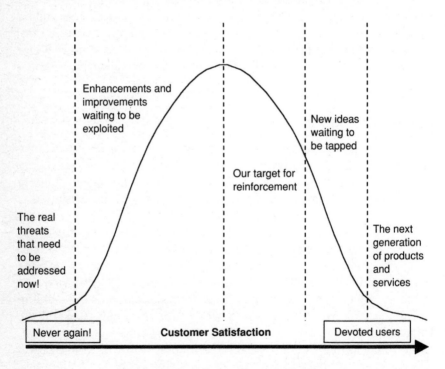

Figure 1.3   *Customer continuum*

CASE STUDY 1.3

In the early 1980s a middle manager was promoted to take charge of a department of 40 people. They were all mavericks, responsible for servicing the needs of the company's research and development department. They tended to pursue their own interests, most of which at the time revolved around the emerging technology of the personal computer.

At her first section meeting the manager announced that she was going to invite someone along to the next meeting to talk about the work in one of their customer departments (although she was careful not to call it that). The guest came along and the group was subjected to 30 minutes of no-nonsense criticism. After the guest left the group was disdainful.

At the next section meeting another guest gave a presentation, and at the next and the next. After two months the group had stopped being scornful and was beginning to behave rather uncomfortably. After three months, some of the younger members were responding with ideas to tackle the problems that the guests were putting forward. After six months the section was unrecognizable. For the first time people in other sections were asking for transfers into it!

After a year the section was awarded the company's performance medal, normally given to an individual. And the section head? She was promoted three times faster than normal. This is the power of customer feedback.

INHIBITING FACTORS

However, there will always be factors that inhibit creative solutions in organizations. These include the following:

- It seems everyone is united in their view that detailed plans and technical specifications hamper, rather than encourage, creative solutions.
- Even major innovative projects such as the feats achieved by Isambard Kingdom Brunel were almost entirely those of one person who designed, and then adapted them, as the project progressed. Despite this, core projects in many companies seem to involve a complete replica of the entire hierarchy.
- Optimal solutions may work, but they take an eternity to achieve. Sub-optimal answers can often be reworked or adapted quicker than waiting for the definitive solution.

- The same quick fix and later reworking argument applies to 'integrated systems'. It is rarely worth the wait for the fully integrated approach to pay back.
- We've already attacked the idea of high technology answers. There are often simpler solutions available that will do the job just as satisfactorily.

NOTES

1   Toffler, A (1970) *Future Shock*, Bantam, New York

2   Belbin, R M (1981) *Management Teams: Why they succeed or fail*, Heinemann, Oxford

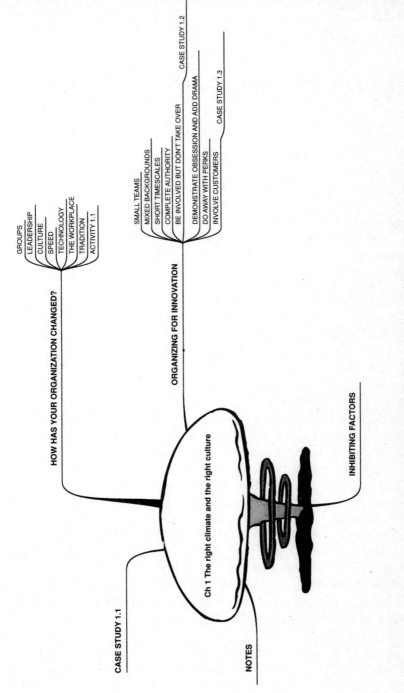

Figure 1.4 *Overview of Chapter 1*

CHAPTER 2

More than one mission

There appear to be a whole range of problems within organizations, and perhaps across whole industries, that revolve around conflicts of 'mission'.

MISSION

What do we mean by 'mission'? For years, strategy consultants have been encouraging the leaders in organizations to define their corporate mission. There are a lot of definitions of the word 'mission' itself. A working one might be around some common purpose that the organization is trying to achieve. Thus a police force might define its mission as the 'protection of people and property'. A fire fighting force might define its as 'rapid response fire and rescue service', and so on.

The people consultants then get hold of this definition and suggest that it has to be motivating to work there, so simply saying what we do isn't good enough. People take pride in being better than the rest so the organization should aim to excel at what it does. Hence the university that claims to be 'providing citizens of the future with more opportunities than any other seat of learning'.

Finally, the marketers put in their contribution. Not only must the mission describe what we do, and do so in terms that inspire us to be the best, but also do so in an imaginative fashion. So, the RAC became 'New Knights of the Road' and the AA became 'The Fourth Emergency Service'.

It doesn't take a great deal of thought to see that there are all sorts of potential conflicts created by mission statements, but this is only part of the problem that we shall look at here. Clearly, how the senior managers in an organization choose to describe it is sensibly up to them. There are all sorts of issues that might lead them to select a particular set of words. However, their choice does have to be credible and communicable. Of the examples I've mentioned so far, perhaps the most problematic is the university one. It says some important things – the focus on the 'citizens of the future', the word 'providing', and the idea that it is 'providing opportunities' are all capable of provoking thought. Whether they can really substantiate the claim to provide more than any other place is open to interpretation and no doubt they have some statistic to justify this. Their credibility might not be 100 per cent, but the real problem here is with communicability. The statement is long, and it requires quite a lot of thought and interpretation for an employee to see how it relates to their own job.

Activity 2.1

Perhaps this is an obvious activity, but it is worth doing with a little care. First, write down your own organization's mission. Does it have one clearly defined? Has it been changed? If so, chart the history of its evolution.

Now also try to record the missions of the various organizations with which you are associated. What about professional bodies? Do you belong to any bodies outside work? What is the 'mission' of the clubs, societies, associations, and so on that you belong to? It isn't perfect, but if they don't have one, look at their motto. Sometimes these give a better insight into the purpose of the organization than you might imagine. My old school had the motto 'slow but sure' – in Latin, of course! Another body that I'm a member of has the graphic phrase 'Whomsoever you see in distress, recognize in him a fellow man'.

Jot down all of these different statements. We shall use them later in this chapter and in Chapter 6.

A 'SENSE' OF MISSION

The next set of problems with 'missions' is how the mass of employees can be helped to gain a 'sense' of mission. We mean by this that they can all understand what the mission is about, and relate it directly to their own job. But more than that – the employees need to be able to share that sense at an emotional level.

To feel such an affinity there has to be something in the mission that really 'sparks' with the individual. It has to relate to them, to why they want to get up each day and go to work, to some inner drive. This may sound very difficult to achieve, yet for many organizations the very fact that certain people have chosen to work for them says something about that person's values and how they tie in to those of the organization. It probably didn't take much for the AA to align its roadside patrols to the 'Fourth Emergency Service' concept. This is not just a motley collection of car mechanics, nor is it a band of aspiring Formula 1 drivers, nor indeed of automotive engineers the likes of which you would find in a Volkswagen, Ford or Volvo factory. We can be fairly certain that the 'appeal' of the job has something to do with the dimensions of being 'on call', of 'rescue', of 'public service', and so on.

However, there are many problems in companies where the 'mission' is dreamt up in an isolated place, and no effort is made to engender the sense of purpose that we are describing. As a minimum, it needs adequate communication, and the opportunity for groups of employees to discuss it and what it implies. In some organizations local versions are created as part of this process, to try to capture the specific needs of this particular group. For instance, we worked with a chemical company whose mission was clearly defined but couldn't seem to gain the proactive support of the R&D group based elsewhere in the country. Rather than simply adopt the mission for manufacturing and leave R&D to sort themselves out, we were asked to find out what the problem might be and do something to alleviate it. We found a group of 450 employees who had never visited the manufacturing plant so couldn't really understand what it did. There was a historical legacy of under-investment in R&D for anything but direct costs – so their canteen was tatty, the buildings were last painted years before, there were no company cars for managers, training was restricted to managerial skills, and so on. Creating a sense of mission is about either changing or reaffirming the culture of the organization. It requires investment, involvement and individual insight. Failing to achieve any of these leads to all kinds of institutional 'cultural' problems.

Activity 2.2

For each of the organizations that you considered in the previous activity, what has been done to create a shared sense of mission among those who have the same affiliation? The charity I mentioned earlier draws heavily on the image of people in distress in their promotional literature. The director general writes about the theme in the foreword to their annual report and most of their publications. The motto is on all their insignia and awards. The basic level of entrance to the organization includes an examination, of which one of the common questions is about the motto.

PERSONAL 'MISSION'

So we come to the really exciting, but also very tough, bit! In the previous sections I've alluded to people having a personal mission though I haven't said so explicitly. For some people, a sense of personal mission is strong – they are very clear about what is important to them and how they are going to achieve it. They don't waste their time on questions about the role they play or with whom. This doesn't mean that our personal missions can't change. Quite the opposite. It is common for them to change through time as we go through different stages in our lives. More on that in Chapters 6 and 7. For the moment we'd like you to start thinking about yourself; by doing so you are more likely to see the kinds of conflict that arise for others over issues of mission.

Activity 2.3

To what extent can you describe your own 'mission'? What is it in your life that gives you a buzz?

This isn't an easy question to answer, so don't try to do so instantly. Try thinking over what you do on a day-to-day, week-by-week basis and see what sorts of things you have done for a long time and seem to excite you, or hold your attention and interest. Don't be afraid if nothing instantly comes to mind or if what does seems too 'daft' to mention.

I met someone a little while ago who said that her passion was her children. Work was merely a means of earning a living. What is it about the children? What is it that you enjoy with them that is so great?

There's bound to be some things that are not so fantastic, so try honing your definition.

A colleague is a lively presenter on training courses but can also facilitate groups well too. When he asked himself this question recently he immediately said that he enjoyed entertaining people. This didn't explain the facilitation process. He thought more carefully and said that actually he enjoyed being a bit of a subversive in the organizations he worked with. How? Well he would help people say things and draw conclusions that they would never have dared say before. We explored this a bit further and he began to see that in doing so he was actually wanting to achieve more radical change yet felt that he couldn't as he was engaged to 'toe the line' of whatever change process the organization was introducing.

There are no rules that the answer has to be a simple one. But don't over-complicate it if you don't have to. Don't expect all parts of your life to be as exhilarating either. If you can, try keeping notes for a few days to see if anything new comes to mind.

Right now, it is time to consider what you expected out of working where you do. When you joined the organization, or your last one if you are not currently working, what did you expect to get out of working there?

Give some thought also to aspects of your life outside work. What do you enjoy at home and in your leisure time? Are there consistent interests in the literature that you read, the movies you go to see, the dreams you have of 'one day...'. And what are the fantasies that you have on holiday?

We shall pick this theme up in Chapter 6.

THE 'HIDDEN' MISSION

There are some jobs that make many people ask, from time to time, why does anyone do that for the money? For example, why do nurses put up with the conditions in which they often work, the hours that they work, the low pay that they receive, and the limited kudos that they receive generally?

For many organizations it seems that there is a 'hidden' mission that the work is fulfilling for the employees. A clue to this can often be gleaned by looking at the common backgrounds of the people that work there, both in terms of how they trained and their childhood, schooling and early work experience.

The operational staff of one of the major international hotel groups entered the industry straight from school, either getting a job in the hotels or going to hotel school and then into the industry. At an early age, they left home and went to work somewhere that would give them accommodation, food and camaraderie, in a very structured and precise environment. While the 'mission' of the group speaks of hospitality, international travelling and customer service, the 'hidden' mission of the group is about providing a home and family for their staff. By understanding both the overt and the hidden missions we can manage the organization and any change within it in a much more effective manner.

A fire and rescue service also offers a very structured environment, where people serve in extraordinary, frightening conditions, helping people who are often completely terrified. The recruits come from a variety of backgrounds but predominantly three: exceptionally almost straight from school; from the armed forces; or after several attempts to find a career in civilian life. The structure that they receive, the disciplined environment, proving themselves time and time again in situations that are so extreme, all call for a similar personality – often one that has not been recognized much at home; there may have been a lot of instability in the family, and perhaps either it didn't seem to have any rules or, more likely, the rules (however unfair) were at least clear. The hidden mission is about reaffirming that rules are fair and have a purpose, that each individual has something very worthwhile to contribute and that your team will not let you down.

CASE STUDY 2.1

One High Street chain of travel agents has a small kiosk in each branch that offers foreign exchange. This is a simple sign that the branch isn't just somewhere to buy a holiday but it is also somewhere to handle money. Indeed, money handling is really their mission. They are a small subsidiary of a major multinational bank and they do make their money out of handling money, whether it is foreign exchange, travellers cheques, money transmission, or insurance. However, ask their staff what they do and you'll find that providing people with holidays, travel, glamour, excitement, and foreign adventure all feature in their views of the mission. The staff joined a travel agency and instead found themselves working in a bank! Now what might the hidden mission be of this organization? Many of the employees have had extensive travel experience before joining. They often left home in their late teens and went around the world or would have if their finances had allowed. They have often worked abroad or else in the leisure or tourist industries in the United Kingdom and some have even worked in the travel trade while working abroad! Why do people travel? There must be lots of reasons but among them is the desire to find something that is otherwise missing, to escape into an expansive world, to be stimulated. Now few of these are things that you would associate with banking. So it isn't surprising that the bank has difficulty managing, motivating and keeping these people. Inevitably it assumed that if they left they could be replaced with more suitable people – those who liked the banking environment. But why do customers go into a travel agency? It isn't usually to handle money! So now the customers are being served by people who are more interested in getting their hands on the money and aren't really at all excited by the prospect of foreign travel in dusty climes with people and situations that can't be predicted!

I'm sure that you'll have begun to see some of the nightmarish consequences of failing to take into account the two different missions.

Activity 2.4

Now look at yourself and your organization. What kinds of things do you have in common with the people there? Does the organization share something in common with your past? For example, have cars featured strongly in your life, or foreign travel perhaps? Have you always had a love of something and now find yourself working with it? What led you into this job, this industry, and this organization? If you are tempted to say, 'by chance' be careful. Though that is possible it is also extremely rare. We may not consciously ask for a job somewhere but we can still gravitate there even if the decisions were taken by default.

What kinds of conclusions can you begin to draw about the hidden mission of your organization?

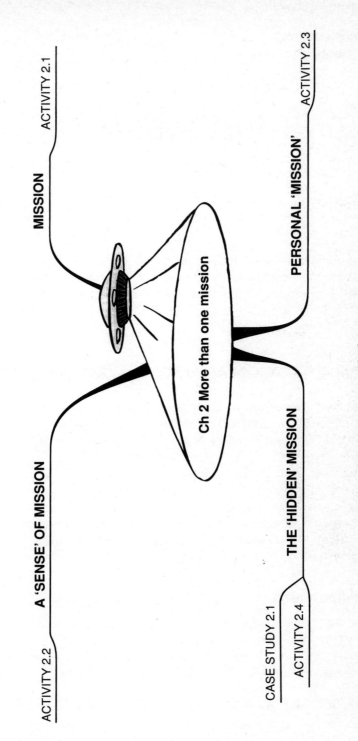

ACTIVITY 2.1

MISSION

A 'SENSE' OF MISSION

ACTIVITY 2.2

Ch 2 More than one mission

PERSONAL 'MISSION'

ACTIVITY 2.3

THE 'HIDDEN' MISSION

CASE STUDY 2.1

ACTIVITY 2.4

Figure 2.1 *Overview of Chapter 2*

CHAPTER 3

Communication

For some strange reason, communication seems to be a perennial problem for organizations. Whether it is about miscommunication, special communication needs (like a major organizational change) or the handling of a serious incident, communication problems seem to crop up regularly.

COMMUNICATION AS AN ORGANIZATIONAL PROBLEM

We aren't concerned directly here with individual communication – the problems that occur when two people are talking to one another. That said, it is worth considering how many people are really involved in the 'problem'. For example, we often find ourselves in a discussion with a senior manager in a company who is describing a breakdown in communication concerning a group of employees. When we get them to break this population down into groups and then to say how many are involved at each stage, it is surprising how often there are only two or three individuals concerned!

Ad hoc needs

A lot of problems appear to be due to *ad hoc* needs. For example, a new factory is to open, the management team is wrapped up in the excitement of the new opportunity it represents and publicly announces the benefits. They fail to reflect on the current employees at other locations and how they might receive the news. Does it signal the closure of their own plant? Can the company really sell sufficient products to match the capacity of both plants? Will the skills of the new workforce be such that they eventually take the jobs of the old ones? Within a few days, the good news story has appeared in the press as a sour backlash and a communication problem exists. Even handled properly, the communication of a critical event is a 'problem' that needs to be solved.

A culture of communication

The second set of issues revolves around the desire to create and sustain a culture of communication. Don't ignore the fact that many so-called 'cultural changes', such as those of the knowledge organization, the learning company, high performance teams, total quality, and so on, all include an expectation of a highly communicative culture. Often attempts to introduce these cultures focus on the practical deliverables rather than the communication culture that needs to be in place for the deliverables to be realized.

Two cultural aspects of communication that have received a lot of publicity in the past are worth remembering: management by walking about (MBWA) and team briefing.

MBWA

Immortalized by Tom Peters, the concept of 'managing by wandering around' is simple – spend more time with your employees, speaking to them, listening to their difficulties and using your skills, authority and ability to cross boundaries to resolve them or put the people who can in touch.

As a basic management philosophy it would be tough to find something better. In practice, some managers find this idea appealing and easy to do. I recall speaking to one who said that he couldn't imagine a day going by without him spending at least an hour or so walking about the shop floor. Another decided to close his office in the HQ, invested in a state-of-the-art mobile phone and fax and spent the working week travelling from one site to another.

Sadly, perhaps, this isn't the natural style for many managers. Often, it seems, pressures from outside prevent them from getting out from behind their desks and speaking to anyone other than their PA. At 6.30 in the evening they realize that it's time to go home and that they have missed meeting anyone. As they leave the office block they say goodbye to the security guard who is probably the only person that knows them very well. Even in a small professional practice, it is easy to sit back and suddenly realize that the day has gone and people have started going home before you found the time to turn to them and ask how their day was going.

I often wonder how many organizational communication problems could be resolved if the culture of asking people how they are and how they are doing could be created. Simple but effective.

Team briefing

Something that was strongly advocated by the Industrial Society was the practice of formal, *downward*, communication sessions held regularly, attended by all employees and conducted by means of a prescribed cascade. It seems that some companies adopted this practice, evolved their own version and have stuck to it for years. Others have tried it and dropped it quickly, while some have said it simply isn't for them.

The team briefing process is a good one for organizations interested in systematically improving the quality of communication internally and whether you adopt it yourselves or not, there's a lot to be learnt from the early practitioners.

SOME MYTHS

Communication seems to be dominated by misperceptions and myths. These range from simple things like the perceived cost of producing different forms of communication, to their effectiveness. The myths include stereotyping of the audiences, fantasies about the dangers of giving information, and so on. Here are a few of the popular ones.

Myth no. 1: They won't understand

Our staff are so stupid, so ignorant, so ill-educated, that they couldn't possibly understand what we are talking about.

So, how did you get to understand it? What did you do to acquire the skills, experience and knowledge to understand it? Was this something that happened today, last week, last month, last year, in the first week that you started work? Are you saying that they can't follow the argument, can't handle the figures, and can't grasp the concepts?

Then you need to be sure that you are right. After all, many of the country's politicians worked on the shop floor, left school at 15, packed boxes, stacked shelves, polished floors or whatever and now look at them – they're running a much bigger corporation that you are!

If you are right (and personally I doubt it), then it is up to you to find a way of communicating that 'they' will understand. But be warned – woe betide you if you end up over-simplifying or patronizing!

Myth no. 2: They'll react the 'wrong' way

There's a good deal of truth in this. After all, when Taylor's scientific methods were introduced in factories in the United States and France in the early years of the 20th century, the employees not only went on strike, they rioted to such an extent that an Act of Congress and a similar decree in France had to be passed banning the methods from further use. Appalling, isn't it? Such a simple change in working practices could have maximized production output, improved efficiency, reduced costs and dramatically grown profits. The price might have been a few people ending up doing mindless tasks repetitively for hours on end and with no respite except for the end of hours bell, but why should we worry about that?

It seems that adverse reactions like this happen because people have been persistently ill informed or kept out of the picture for years on end. Suddenly they are presented with the 'facts' and they rebel. On the other hand, where people have been well informed, given raw information rather than glossy versions, and asked for their understanding of it, with ideas for addressing it, the results are usually way beyond the expectations of the managers who had previously kept them out of the picture. One company in the construction industry adamantly refused to share financial data with the employees. When they eventually had to because redundancies were looming and there were fears of the adverse publicity, the response was to introduce new working terms and conditions that did away with overtime, reduced the hourly rate of pay, and paid on performance. The idea for this extraordinary change did not come from the managers – it came from the employees themselves.

CASE STUDY 3.1

A clothing manufacturer, selling many of their lines to well-known High Street shops, recently suffered from a quality problem. The result was the postponement or outright cancellation of several orders including some from a particularly significant customer. For weeks, the management team struggled to resolve the problems and to salvage the relationships that had been so badly hurt. They resisted any thoughts of involving the customers as they felt that these people wouldn't understand the technicalities of what they were doing, would see only confusion and chaos, were likely to cancel even more orders and could lead to the collapse of the business. Requests for information and on-site appointments from the customer were parried off with vague excuses and sluggish responses – driven by these fears.

After nearly six weeks, a car arrived at the site entrance. The occupants were two former employees, who now worked as technical managers for the customer. They had no appointment but refused to go unless they could meet the production manager or his assistant and tour the plant. An extraordinary standoff took place in the reception area. Eventually, and very reluctantly, the MD agreed to them coming on-site. Neither of the production managers was available, so the MD, accompanied by a junior technical adviser, conducted the site tour. The adviser was far more forthcoming in his responses to their questions than the MD would have liked. When they saw the real reason for the problems – some old machinery that was proving almost impossible to calibrate properly at high speed – the two visitors suggested some simple experiments to establish the capability of the machinery and identify optimal settings. The adviser was delighted – their knowledge was no better than his but they had an outsider's perspective that questioned some of the assumptions that had been made by the production managers.

The customer eventually acquired the manufacturer, invested in new equipment and trained the employees in problem solving and production experimentation. The only people to be made redundant in the takeover were the management team.

Myth no. 3: They'll tell the competitors

A fascinating example of this fear emerged when a company was trying to implement self-managed teams. The teams needed detailed production costs and advance order information to make scheduling decisions. The managers were very concerned about this, as they said that the employees might give it to competitors.

No one asked why they would be so daft as to do something that might make them lose their jobs. It took a brave HR director to point out that he had never heard of employees coming to them with competitor information, but that it was one of their principal recruiting decisions when they took on a senior manager: 'What useful information will they have about the competition?'.

THE AUDIENCE

Perhaps the most obvious, yet often overlooked, step is to ask who the audience of the communication needs to be. Even for what appears to be an entirely internal issue, there can sometimes be advantages in including external people. Similarly, for an event that might seem to be externally focused, it can be worth copying in (at the very least) the employees.

For example, a government body was going through enormous restructuring. The result was bound to be job losses. Job losses do not look good for any government, and the media especially could be expected to respond with glee! So there needed to be some kind of public as well as internal communication. The management team anticipated an adverse reaction from the union representatives. The resulting communication plan included several distinct audiences: the ministers directly responsible and their colleagues right up to Prime Ministerial level; the unions locally and at national level (in fact, they even extended to some influential foreign union leaders); the employees, past as well as present; the editors of several newspapers and magazines; conference organizations and some of the lobbying professional organizations such as the Institute of Directors and the Confederation of British Industry; related bodies, which included the Bank of England and HM Customs and Excise, and so on. For each audience, a detailed plan was drawn up, the characteristics of the audience and the likely interest or 'angle' they would take was anticipated. For each, an effort was made to foresee their own perspective on the issues – who would they then communicate with, who should know before them, who should they know in advance of, what level of contact would they expect, and so on. Once these plans had evolved, they were rationalized to make the best use of the resources available and to minimize the risks of both duplication and the sequences going wrong. Disaster plans were drawn up: if, for example, the press said 'X', how would it be handled and how would the other audiences be addressed? The result was one of the smoothest transitions in government re-engineering. Although there were undoubtedly mistakes in the re-engineering itself, at no time did a difficulty arise because of communication failure.

Activity 3.1

To help make this chapter 'real' you might like to list your own internal audiences. There's obviously the management team and the front-line workforce. You might include distributors and agents here or externally. Depending on the circumstances, you might include key professional advisers, such as auditors, lawyers and media advisers. What about the internal functions? Are the needs of the marketing department or the HR function different from those of the production or distribution groups?

Without over-generalizing, can you define them more precisely? How do they differ from one another? Are the head office functions almost entirely graduates while the production staff are from non-English speaking backgrounds, for example?

Spend a few moments reflecting on the different ways that these groups get their information. A predominantly young workforce will tend to read certain kinds of magazine, attend certain kinds of events, and so on. An older workforce may read different things, not just in content but also in style. If you are serious about finding the best means of reaching your audience then go out and buy examples, look at the way they are laid out, the type of article, its style of language and length. These are clues to the kind of communication medium that you need to use.

Will one style cover all your needs? You might want to adopt different ones for different groups. One biscuit manufacturer in the north of England has a mixed workforce – roughly half the employees are from Pakistani families and the other half are from Anglo-Saxon ones. The staff newsletter is deliberately produced in a combination of styles and languages to reflect the two groups. Particularly important articles appear in two languages, while others appear in one or the other. There is a fascinating buzz in the canteen on days when a new magazine appears as the Pakistani employees explain to the others what they have missed and vice versa. In the past there was virtually no mixing of the two groups away from the line, today there is far more.

Another good example of matching styles to different populations comes from one of the large contract catering firms. Their general staff monthly is styled after the popular celebrity magazine, *Hello!* The managerial one is based on a similar appearance to *Management Today*.

CASE STUDY 3.2

One petrol company wanted to improve the safety performance of their tanker drivers. At the same time they realized that these people were the face of the company to many of their customers – the owners and managers of the petrol stations. The first person who would be asked about the company, or some development within it, was the tanker driver. But how could these drivers best be communicated with? The drivers frequently listened to local radio as they were doing their rounds. So the company contracted a well-known radio presenter to produce a monthly magazine tape with company and product news, driving tips from racing drivers, the Institute of Advanced Motorists, the police, and so on, together with interviews with individual drivers themselves about things that they did outside the company, all interspersed with popular music.

Activity 3.2

Having tried to identify your internal audiences, do the same for the ones outside the company. Suppliers, customers, consumers, shareholders and the local community, are all examples. Again, consider how they normally get their information and see what common characteristics they might have.

Ask yourself who these people respect. As with the tanker drivers, getting a widely respected individual to contribute can be the key to maximizing the amount of information that people retain, which is often the most important aspect of the communication process.

THE CONTENT

Again, the content depends on the purpose of the communication. If this is a one-off, special piece of news, then you probably won't want to confuse it with other items and besides, most people will be keen to know what you have to say. On the other hand, if you have regular snippets to impart but want to hold attention, you might be better giving space to material of more 'human' interest to encourage people to even open the magazine or whatever.

Do not over-simplify your message, but equally don't put so much in that you leave no stone unturned. Most good communications give a brief summary and then refer people to another source for more detail. This can be a far cheaper medium, such as a staff-only Web site, or it can be produced in smaller quantities and only sent to those that request it.

WHICH MEDIUM?

To a certain extent the decision as to which medium to use for your messages will be determined by the same constraints as all the other decisions around communication – urgency, timing, resources, material, and so on.

The printed word

Obviously, a popular choice for many years has been the printed word. Letters can be sent to individuals at work or at their home, simple A4 news pages can be distributed personally or made available at the site entrance or exit. Magazines can be made to cover both internal and external needs or devoted to one or another sector. Posters can be displayed at key points and may be much cheaper than a letter sent individually.

If you have any doubts about your audience's ability to read for whatever reason, then think twice before using this approach which could anger and alienate rather than inform.

The spoken word

Using group briefings or discussion groups, whole company meetings, celebrations, open days, and one-to-one sessions are all ways of communicating by voice rather than print. Obviously they can allow greater spontaneity, provide room for questions to be asked and for people to challenge. If you are comfortable with this, then you'll be happy doing so. If you are not comfortable working in this kind of environment, then avoid it!

The chief executive of a large company received universal acclaim for his ability to captivate a large audience. His managers and staff relished one-to-one conversations with him. Yet he had problems with his management team – particularly in getting them to work together as a team rather than constantly fighting one another. His forte was definitely not in small groups and for him it was better to either avoid them or improve his ability to work in them. Another CEO was a complete contrast – fine one-to-one, a great motivator in a small team, but terrified of working with large audiences. We are all different and we should choose our medium according to our strengths or do something about our weaknesses.

The spoken word doesn't have to be restricted to face-to-face or live performances. We've already mentioned the tanker drivers and their tapes.

Video

The MD of one holiday firm spent a fortune on a company video. It was distributed widely across all the operating divisions of the company. In it a famous journalist interviewed him about his plans for the company. Bold statements, strong messages, and not a sound of conviction in his voice once. Quite the opposite – it sounded as if he had been reading from a script – which, of course, he had, just 'out of camera'. It took less than three months from the distribution of the video to his early retirement.

He couldn't have been further removed from the reality of his employees. His successor was advised by all the other directors not to make another company video. But he did. This time, it was a cleverly edited 10-minute programme that captured members of the staff – at all levels – in candid interviews asking them what they considered the future of the company to be. He toured the country, presenting the video, followed by a discussion, followed by a 10-minute presentation by him. The company's 17 sites were visited within 10 days – two, sometimes three, programmes each day. The MD went from obscurity to being a widely respected and well-known champion of the staff almost overnight. The full presentation – all three parts – were recorded and edited again as a video. The cost was much less than many people expected. Copies were offered to all shareholders, to journalists, to suppliers, to new recruits and for nearly 12 months it formed part of the company induction programme for its many seasonal staff. After a year, he repeated the process. This time he even had some ex-employees interviewed. Why had they left? One nearly cried, as she'd had to leave because of family commitments. Another had been offered a great job elsewhere for more money. Another had decided to travel abroad before going to university. In his face-to-face presentation he addressed each reason – from now on, staff would be offered subsidized crèches, staff who left for extended leave and who had a good performance record would be given first priority when applying for a job on their return. Staff leaving for higher education (and bear in mind that a lot of students worked here as seasonal employees) would receive a one-off £100 gift towards their books. Again, the composite video was offered to any interested parties. Within a year, the HR department reported that staff turnover was at an all-time low, that recruitment costs were a fraction of the level two years previously, and the majority of junior managers had experience of working for the company on the front line.

Satellite

When the target audience is widely distributed, perhaps even globally, and the message is considered time-sensitive, then satellite can even be used. One motor manufacturer, keen to improve the technical and company knowledge, affinity, and skills of their salespeople worldwide, produced a 20-minute programme for broadcast at the weekend every fortnight. It was beamed out from three satellites covering the globe and recorded by timed video recorders in the showrooms regardless of the time of day or night that it was broadcast. The programme was entirely graphic, with a simple voiceover being used in the languages of the recipients. The resulting combination was viewed and listened to in the showrooms on Tuesday morning.

Electronic-based media

Perhaps the most exciting development in communication media of late has been the Internet and other electronic forms. Simple use of technology has been a boon in all sorts of companies. For example, one motor plant near Detroit has an intranet Web site that carries a combination of company, plant, employee, and community news. There's a simple bulletin board for employee discussions and another for classified advertisements. The discussion one focuses on both work-related and general issues and appears as a scrolling message on screens placed around the works. When President Clinton was being harangued for his alleged extra-marital affairs, the debate on the bulletin flourished. It spanned not only his situation but also morality generally, issues of media intrusion, emotional needs of couples in relationships, different needs of heterosexual and gay couples, and the contrasting religious perspectives on marriage, sex and commitment. What has this got to do with the company and isn't it detracting people from their real work? Hardly. As one of the company vice-presidents commented: 'Participating in a structured dialogue like this is improving people's ability to present reasoned arguments, it's educating them on moral issues, bringing diversity into real life, enriching their understanding and ability to work with their colleagues... Oh, and it's teaching them to use computers in a rapid and unprescribed way. All told, it's our single best spend on education and training!'

Today, most computer networks provide simple communication tools of this kind. The Internet allows both public and password-controlled sites so employees can have their own 'channel'. E-mail allows messages to be sent out to everyone simultaneously.

The only downside, at the moment, is that even in the most high-tech company there are some employees who don't have access to the company systems. One company recently discovered that there was a big 'us and them' divide emerging because messages were being distributed by e-mail which could only be obtained by managers and secretaries as they were the only people to have e-mail facilities. A simple oversight but one that took a lot of effort to resolve.

Another electronic aid that is often forgotten is the mobile phone. Many people in the United Kingdom have a mobile phone and elsewhere the pager is more common. Most of these can be used to receive 'short messages'. The cost of sending the messages depends on the billing structure but isn't usually borne by the receiver. A few smart companies are using automated technology to send staff a short message when something significant happens during the day. One, for example, is a rail company. They notify ALL staff who have advised them of their mobile phone numbers, with a short message, if a train is delayed, if there has been an accident, if a member of staff has achieved something significant, and so on. When a train was held up recently because of an accident along the line, the short message asked any member of staff travelling on this particular train to liaise with the conductor to help resolve any onward travel problems for the passengers. This nearly impossible task for the conductor was achieved smoothly when nearly a dozen other employees who happened to be on the train stepped in and helped out for half an hour.

THE PROCESS

The simple, yet most powerful, lesson that we have learnt over the years about communication in organizations revolves around process rather than content. In particular, around the design process more than the delivery one. It has two parts; always appoint someone who is to be co-ordinator and always involve a cross-section of interested parties.

If the process is left to volunteers, or it is seen as a peripheral adjunct to 'real work', then it will soon disintegrate to nothing. Someone has to be given the responsibility to make it happen. This can be someone from almost any part of the business – it doesn't have to be a manager, a secretary, an HR professional, a marketing person or whatever.

The editor of the motor plant Web site mentioned earlier, is one of the site electricians. She was interested in doing something different, initially volunteered to be involved in the project, discovered ways of making HTML (the universal Web site language) 'sing' and so was asked if she would spend the equivalent of a day a week editing and running the programme. She introduced the bulletin boards, suggested the site-wide screens, acts as moderator if contributions become too 'hot' and now promotes the idea by travelling to other company sites advising them on how to set up similar facilities.

If just one person drives the process, whether in deciding the content, the medium, the timing or whatever, then there is a good chance that it will fall short of the mark. This isn't a question of commitment, as even the MD will fall foul if they try to take it on themselves. It is all about understanding the audience and developing something that people will really want and use. A small team, including people from the target audience, will be able to identify what will work and what won't. They can give advice on the readability and style of the material. They will ask the awkward questions that are being glossed over. They will pour scorn on the trivializing elements and gimmicks.

TIMING

Deciding how often to provide one-directional information, like a newsletter, involves assessing the urgency, cost, effort, sources of material, and so on. Often problems arise because commitment is made to production more often than the material or resources allow. It is often better to be frugal and stick to your commitment than to appear to fall short.

A quarterly document well done is far better than a weekly done badly. That said, it is now so easy to publish information through a Web site that you can achieve far more for less effort and much more frequently.

Pay particular attention to coordinating the publication with other events. For instance, you might time a newsletter to coincide with a seminar or workshop. But do you do so before, at the same time or afterwards? Each has its own advantages and the decision will depend on your own unique circumstances.

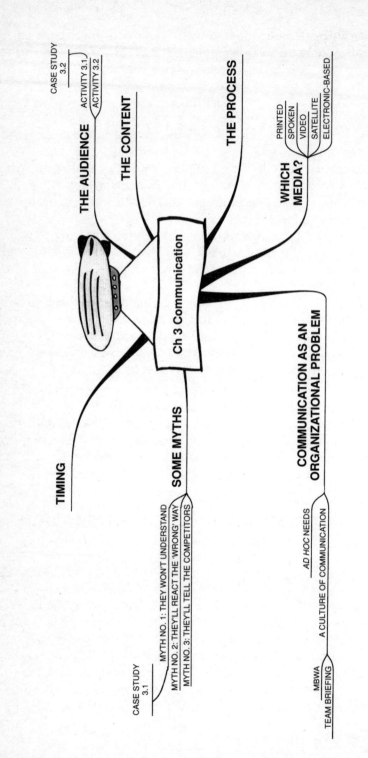

Figure 3.1   *Overview of Chapter 3*

CHAPTER 4

Achieving results through small groups

Try to read this chapter in two ways. In one sense it tries to look at the nitty-gritty of tackling a problem using a group. Groups of people are hotbeds of relationships, and as relationships are at the bottom of most problems at work, the group that you try to use is likely to have almost as many problems as it is trying to resolve! So this is a chapter about how your problem-solving group may work and some of the problems that may arise within it.

You may not have a problem-solving group. It is more than likely that you are looking at this chapter because you have a group that has problems and you are looking at ways to resolve them. Either way, I hope that you'll find it useful.

TEAMS ARE SO MUCH TROUBLE, WHY BOTHER?

Why teams?

Why is there so much interest in teams? Why do some organizations not only make the basic structure of their business the team and then allow them to be self-directed? The question is more why did they ever stop using teams? After all, there's plenty of evidence of team structures in animal and primitive human societies.

Many people work in teams as often as they can. Outside work there are many opportunities to do so: sports, community action, political, charity, youth, councils and professional bodies. In almost every case the unit of organization is the group.

Despite the predominance of team working in our society, the educational system almost entirely encourages individual-centred (some would say self-centred) development. In the United Kingdom virtually the only team-oriented school activities are games lessons. Throughout their school life most children and especially adolescents risk punishment for displaying a team orientation: they are either ostracized for belonging to a gang or penalized for cheating in assessed activities. Whether this is the reason that so many academic failures make good business people would be an excellent topic for an MBA thesis, but it is outside the scope of this book!

Using teams to tackle problems is far less threatening to senior managers than completely restructuring the organization. As discussed elsewhere, problem-solving teams often act as a catalyst for the general transition to teams by demonstrating the power of team working.

So why teams? In short, they tend to produce more cost-effective and efficient solutions to problems than individuals working in isolation. They can bring a broader range of expertise to a decision. They tend to regulate themselves more thoroughly than an individual. Because they have shared in developing the solution they have greater ownership of the outcome. Because of this shared ownership there are fewer axes to be ground by non-participants. But there is also something collective that leads to greater productivity and more fun among team participants.

Most people are familiar with the concept of the hierarchy of needs proposed by Abraham Maslow,[1] which proposes that what motivates people is fulfilling progressively higher levels of need. Maslow's hierarchy is shown in Figure 4.1.

It is easy to see that the three higher levels, self-actualization, respect and approval and sense of belonging are all more readily achieved in a team than alone. Interaction between team members, whether work related or social, makes the job more enjoyable and builds cohesiveness. In a small group of people there are opportunities for cooperation, specialization and also protection. Even in human societies, when people are exposed to danger they tend to group together. This instinctive behaviour can often be seen among poorly trained troops and was exploited in both the Falklands and Gulf conflicts.

Not only do teams have more fun, but they are also more productive. A comprehensive survey of over 120 different experiments

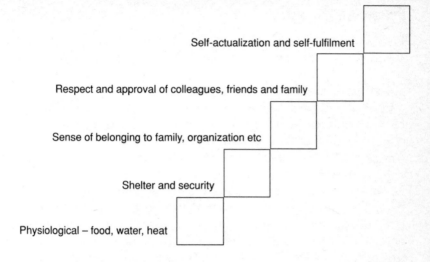

Figure 4.1 *Maslow's hierarchy of needs*

carried out in the late 1970s, showed that co-operation produces more output than either competition or individual motivation.[2] If the work is able to benefit from cooperation, team working always produces more for less. Teams have lower rates of turnover and absenteeism is lower. The impact is enormous – the reduction in turnover reducing by as much as 75 per cent, for example – that even simple observation quickly reveals problem areas. What is more it is possible to predict with startling accuracy which people will leave, simply by looking to see who is being isolated or rejected by the group.

An example may put this into context. A controlled experiment with bricklayers over an 11-month period showed that those working in a properly constructed team produced 12 per cent more work with 16.5 per cent lower materials cost and lower labour turnover.[3]

Activity 4.1

List the groups to which you and your immediate family belong. How did you come to join and what do you get out of being a member? Try to think beyond the material benefits.

Preparing people

We've already suggested that schools are not the place that most people learn the basics of working in teams. If young people do so, it is usually through out-of-school groups such as scouts and guides movements and other youth groups.

At work we do not generally give people much credit for the out-of-work activities that they are involved in. Even those who are clearly leaders in their community can find themselves denied this role at work. I recently came across an individual on a team leaders course that we were running. He had been sent on the course because he was being considered for promotion to a supervisory role. There were other management programmes but these were considered 'too advanced' for him. Early into the programme it emerged that he was a local youth football coach. Over coffee I discovered that he was also a councillor and chaired the planning committee, but the bombshell was when I learned that he was also an NCO in the reserve forces. If there was someone with talent, commitment and experience that was being ignored then here he was.

Perhaps at work we should begin to take a more holistic approach to the development of our staff and encourage them to share more of their experience from outside to our own benefit. Equally, why don't we see more organizations encouraging their staff to take a more proactive role in the community and so learn skills that we can subsequently put to use? There are many organizations that do this, and there are non-profit-making lobby groups encouraging business to do so, but it remains seen as peripheral to the work of the organization and something of marginal benefit.

In Chapters 6 and 7, we explore the impact of the early environment on an individual and how this conditions their responses to and at work. It is worth reminding ourselves that part of the role of employers is to take the individual that comes to them and help that person become a more effective contributor to society. In return, the employer gets a better worker. Sadly, too often this means relearning lessons from childhood rather than reinforcing them.

To enable people to be more effective calls for an appropriate degree of support. This can range from simply publicizing their efforts to mentoring and coaching them. As part of each individual's personal development plan there should be some consideration as to who they are going to get their support from, when and how. And those supporters need preparing so that they can do a good job too!

PROBLEMS WITHIN SMALL GROUPS

So many problems at work revolve around small groups. The group may be a clearly defined part of the organization or it may be a purely *ad hoc* collection of individuals who happen to have developed a problem among themselves. Problems in this sense can reveal themselves in lots of ways: failing to adopt a new working practice, going on strike or a similar action, bullying, being 'sent to Coventry', and so on. The causes can be obvious or far from obvious; they can seem obvious but actually be extremely complex and hidden, they can be institutional, group or individual in their origin. A real mish-mash of trouble and someone, somewhere, will be expected to do something about it. If you feel that you are that person, stop for a moment and double check. Is it really appropriate for you to do so? Not 'is it your responsibility?' or 'is it your job?' but is it appropriate? Teachers at school have a terribly difficult tightrope to tread daily. When trouble brews, is it better for them to intervene or is it better for them to watchfully let the pupils involved resolve it for themselves? At work you may well find yourself in a similar position. Failing to intervene can lead you into trouble and intervening can make the problem even worse. You have to decide for yourself.

How big is a group? What is said here should apply to any collection of people from two upwards. In practice, in the last section, we were more concerned with groups that are largely independent of other influences, whereas here we are concerned with groups that form the smaller part of a whole.

TASK VERSUS PROCESS

Whenever a group of people meets there are a variety of aspects of the group that will decide how well they will operate together. Some of these will depend on the task that the group is tackling. For example, a council meeting may go without incident until a particularly contentious topic arises. Then the normal decorum may be shattered while people with contrasting views attempt to make their point. So one important factor is the content of the task or *task content* as it is sometimes called.

The people that are present may influence the meeting. The contentious issue at the council meeting might have passed unnoticed if there hadn't been people of different political persuasions present. The second ingredient, then, is the *people content*. Choosing a particular group of people to attend a meeting, screening applicants with a psychometric test, giving an open invitation but holding the meeting at a particular time of day, formally inviting guests or holding the meeting in a public place will all control the people content.

To take the example of the council meeting further, the two groups could handle the contentious topic in different ways. Under some circumstances even the most radical theme can be passed by both groups without a murmur, while on another it could lead to a rebellion. Most people have attended meetings where an agenda item has been expected to cause havoc. The way in which the co-ordinator or chairperson handles the matter can make all the difference to the result. These 'ways in which things are done' are all examples of *process*. Having an agenda, using a flip-chart and keeping minutes are examples of *task process*. Two people coming to a meeting together, where people sit around a table and how one person talks to another are examples of *people process*. Defining the items on an agenda, giving people a briefing document before a meeting and training them in certain problem-solving techniques are all ways of influencing the task process.

Figure 4.2 illustrates the matrix of task and process issues. Whenever a group encounters difficulties, it is worthwhile considering which aspects of the matrix are involved.

TASK CONTENT

The original problem

Occasionally the group finds itself tackling a problem that no longer exists. The problem in this case is an example of task content. Imagine the frustration of a group of people who have made a commitment of time and effort and possibly expense, may even have had to fight the system to be allowed to take part – only to find that their *raison d'être* has disappeared. Three things seem to happen for this to occur:

	Task	People
Content	■ Formal agenda ■ Goals The report produced by the finance department did not contain the information that we expected.	■ Who is doing what to whom Row over new bonus arrangements for office staff – none of them was on the working party.
Process	■ How the task is done Our site WP is not compatible with the head office system so staff trained on one need retraining if they move.	■ How members relate to each other Jim will keep reminiscing in management meetings – now Sarah is refusing to work with him.
Structure → Norms	■ Standard operating procedures We always send a copy of the agenda around before the management meetings and a copy of the minutes afterwards.	■ Recurrent personal relationships and roles Tony and Dave always used to travel to the regional meeting in the same car – it was the best way of getting some quality time together. Of all the sales team they seemed to get on best with one another!

Figure 4.2   *Task versus process*

1. An inadequate brief has been submitted.
2. There is a lone fixer.
3. The goal posts have been shifted.

An inadequate brief
From time to time the brief that the team has prepared, or has had prepared for it, is inadequate. As a result, the team either tackles a project which is too ambitious, or more commonly something that is only a subset of the real problem. It is always worth the team reviewing its brief with someone who is in contact with as much of the organization as possible. In a traditional organization this is often related to seniority, while in businesses with less hierarchy the person could be a co-ordinator of some kind.

The lone fixer

At first this might seem like a *people-content* issue, but the way that it is experienced is in a sense of feeling that there is no point carrying on because the issue is already being fixed (*task content*).

A hazard for any group, one of the benefits of team working is that the members will tend to act conservatively when one individual attempts to grind their axe. However, there is little that anyone can do when someone attempts to tackle the task single-handedly, often from outside.

If this happens, the group should ask why that person was involved in their work in the first place. The reason is often an interpersonal conflict or fear of involving them. As soon as the group learns of the lone fixer's activities they should seek to involve them. This needs to be done in as constructive and tactful a way as possible. They should make sure that the fixer has addressed the whole brief, that the approach that has been used has been consistent and appropriate regardless of whether it has been systematic or unstructured, and that the fixer has been privy to the same information as the group. If there are gaps, the fixer needs to be involved in addressing them. The group should make sure that its contacts among the senior management team are aware of what it is doing and how the fixer and the group differ in their spheres of influence.

Shifting goal posts

Where a group is working to a long timescale, it is common to find that the goal posts have been changed before they can report on their progress. Often the problem arises because of changes affecting the organization as a whole. Everyone gets too involved in the organization-wide issues to worry about the group. All sorts of problems can ensue. The individuals usually report frustration at the waste of their time. If there is one, the management team that initiated the group tends to focus more on the individual's feelings than the problem they were tackling. About the only solution to this that we have come across is for the group to be rigorous in their communication with the most senior members of the organization.

At the end of the day, the group has to remind itself that it is there to deliver something of value to the organization, no matter how frustrated they become.

Time and other resources

Another area of frustration and hence problems within groups is their lack of resources (another example of task content). These problems include: time to meet, space, finance, and enough operational time to try out their solutions. Poor understanding and limited commitment by a line manager can lead to lack of involvement by an individual member. Similarly, individuals may over-commit themselves or be over-committed in their normal work. Lack of progress is then blamed on the group's inability (ie they are undervalued) rather than looking at the lack of time spent on the problem and why this has happened.

The 'problem' can expect to have to compete to remain a priority for its members. The co-ordinator will usually adopt the role of attendance monitor and will follow up people who do not attend to find out the reason. Often people identified by the senior management team as crucial to the group are the ones who are already the most over committed. When absences are threatening to destroy the group, the co-ordinator has to adopt a strong role and demand that everyone attends at least one complete group meeting. At this meeting the problem can be discussed and commitment rekindled, if possible.

PEOPLE CONTENT

Insufficient expertise

Obviously, insufficient expertise is another way in which people content has an impact.

Team roles

The concept of team roles is a powerful one and has cropped up elsewhere in this book. Team roles describe the contribution that people bring to a group regardless of the setting. The study of team roles has been extensive but the one with the widest application has been the work by R Meredith Belbin. Belbin studied students at Henley – The Management College over many years. Using a number of psychometric tests and other personality instruments he created artificial teams and gave them tasks to do. He and his co-workers then observed and recorded the behaviour of and performance of the teams. Eventually they developed a simple questionnaire to help people identify their main strengths in a group and a model of the contributions so that a highly effective and complementary team could be developed.

Belbin's work shows that people's contributions combine aspects of three different dimensions. They may bring with them a wide variety of ideas, thereby being most likely to contribute new approaches to the problem. Alternatively, they may have a strong people focus, being concerned with helping win other people to the group's cause and making new decisions work. The third dimension is a strong task-driven approach. These people are good at getting things done, on time and to budget, without being too concerned with the longevity of the solution. In practice, people don't have just one strength, they have combinations. Belbin identified nine combinations that describe the contribution an individual might bring according to the balance of the three dimensions.

Figure 4.3 shows the make-up of the different roles. Obviously problems arise when there are imbalances in a team. Different skills are likely to be most in demand at different stages in solving a problem. For example, a team that has a lot of Shapers and Plants might have difficulty completing anything. One with no Co-ordinator will risk being diverted into irrelevant areas. Too much people focus may mean serious technical or directional issues remain unsolved.

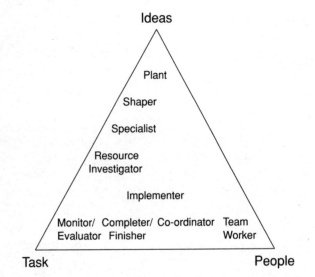

Figure 4.3   *Belbin's team roles in three dimensions*

Activity 4.2

What is your natural role in a group? What roles do the other members of your management team adopt? You may have taken a team roles assessment before, in which case find the results and review them. Alternatively, Table 4.1 shows the characteristics of the various roles with an explanation of each. Using Table 4.1, try assessing your own team – are there any obvious good fits?

There is a lot of value in introducing the whole group to Belbin's work and completing an assessment themselves. You might find it useful to run a separate session looking at the roles people adopt and how they might influence the group.

External experts

Another role that Belbin identified was that of specialist or external expert. He acknowledged that advice will be sought, but didn't explore the problems of using external experts. When you decide to call in an outsider, you are making a decision about the sort of help that you want and the skills of the person that you are bringing in. Figure 4.4 illustrates the three main types of external expert. The difference in their skills and knowledge reflects a fundamental difference in the way they will work with you.

Information provider
Information providers see their role as supplying ideas and additional information, or to provide direct advice based on their experience. They are approached by a group once the group have recognized that a problem exists, have decided on the cause and who they feel is best suited to resolve it.

Even if the information provider is up to date on every aspect of their subject, for him or her to be able to help a number of areas must have been addressed correctly. The team must have made the right diagnosis and they must have correctly assessed the abilities of the information provider. They need to communicate their problem properly and understand the consequences of asking for help, especially if it subsequently emerges that they were wrong in some respect.

This is a common model used by 'one-man' consultancies. The person has relatively unique information and sells it to those who

Table 4.1 *Belbin's team roles – a simplified diagnostic chart*

Role	Characteristics	Contributions	Major strengths	Allowable weaknesses	Common sayings
PLANT/ COMPLETER	Clever, imaginative, unorthodox, serious-minded individual	Original solutions to tough problems, especially early in projects and if off-track	Imagination, intellect, knowledge	Independent, weak communicator, ignores protocol	What about…? I don't have to justify myself to others
RESOURCE INVESTIGATOR	Extrovert, communicative, curious, enthusiastic	Explores opportunities, develop contacts, and negotiate deals	Thinks on feet, sets up outside contacts, great source of energy	Loses interest unless constantly stimulated	I know someone who can… Let me see what I can find
CO-ORDINATOR	Calm, self-confident, mature, controlled, trusting	Motivating to work with, good at clarifying goals, work well in mixed teams	Welcomes others' input without prejudicing	Not usually the cleverest member of a team	So what you're saying is… Has anyone anything to add? Let's keep the goal in sight
SHAPER	Highly motivated, challenging, aggressive	Good manager, very motivating to work with, cuts through politics	Thrives on confrontation, gets teams to produce	Headstrong, emotional, impatient and can offend, may impose pattern on group	No, you're wrong! So what are we going to DO about it?
MONITOR/ EVALUATOR	Sober, unemotional, objective, dry	Good at analysing problems, usually holds key strategic posts	Judgement, discretion	Dry, boring, poor motivator of people	There's always two sides… Let's look out for…
TEAM WORKER	Social, mild, perceptive, sensitive	Most supportive member, prevents people process problems, gets maximum from all	Good listener, well liked, non-threatening	Indecisive and avoids confrontation	Let's give… 's idea some thought. Would you like to add anything else?
IMPLEMENTER	Dutiful, reliable, well organized, enjoy routine	Organizes, turning ideas into actions	Hard working and practical, good organizational ability	Lacks flexibility, resists unproven ideas, slow to respond	We can do… within the budget. Given time we could…
COMPLETER/ FINISHER	Painstaking, orderly, conscientious, appear calm but…	Ideal for tasks needing attention to detail	Fulfils promises and works to high standards	Worries unnecessarily, poor delegator	What about clause 23 on the third page? A stitch in time etc
SPECIALIST	Professional, self-starter, dedicated	Indispensable when local information is crucial	Provides wide-ranging technical knowledge	Shows little interest in others	I'll see what I can find out. We must keep up our standards

The information
provider

Doctor–patient

Process counsellor

Figure 4.4   *Three types of external expert*

call on them. Delivery may be wrapped up in a variety of ways but fundamentally the information is handed out to people who have already made their own diagnosis of the situation.

Doctor–patient

The second style of expert relationship is known as the 'doctor–patient' model. The group turns to the 'doctor' as if it were some kind of 'patient'. It hasn't made the diagnosis, but has observed some symptoms. The doctor makes a diagnosis and then tells the team what to do.

This is a common model used among the larger consultancies. Often a group (which may be a whole company) will approach the consultancy describing a number of symptoms. The consultancy will persuade the company that it needs to gather more information about the symptoms before it can offer any prescription. These data are collected through what is known as a 'diagnostic' phase.

Many assumptions are being made in this situation. The doctor's diagnosis needs to be seen as helpful by the group, which needs to have chosen the right doctor for its symptoms in the first place. This means that the group needs to have recorded its symptoms properly and interpreted them correctly. The doctor's prescription has to be effective and acceptable to the group. The group needs to understand the prescription properly and have the resources and ability to use it.

The doctor–patient style is very common within organizations and relies heavily on shared knowledge of the subject. Unfortunately, teams are notoriously bad at following the prescription. This is a human trait which reflects a lack of ownership for the solution – it is why so many of us do not complete prescriptions for antibiotics!

Process counsellor

The third style of expert is the process counsellor. He or she helps the group to understand what is happening around them and how they can exert influence to achieve their goals. There is no risk of the problem being passed from the group to the process counsellor, as tends to happen with the other styles, since the team is responsible for both the diagnosis and the solution. Process counsellors need not have any direct experience of the problem – their skills are in helping those that do understand it better.

The use of process counsellors is more open-ended than with other experts. They will be particularly effective when there is an unidentified problem that no one is resolving, and when the sort of advice that is needed is far from clear. The group members must want to learn from the problem-solving process and are probably the only people likely to know which solution will work in practice.

Most successful groups have a process counsellor permanently assigned to them. In this case the person is often called a facilitator. This is not a training or leadership role, but one of an outside expert. A fascinating example of the contribution that such people can make can be seen in the Star Trek series, where a process counsellor became a member of the senior management team of the USS Enterprise!

Activity 4.3

What kinds of outside experts does your organization use? How does it select them? If your business is reasonably large (say, over 1,000 employees), you probably use more outsider experts than you realize. To what extent are the different styles understood and appreciated by the people using them?

Involvement

Obviously, if you don't have the right people involved in solving a problem you are likely to run into difficulties. But what makes someone the 'right' person?

Technical
We have already touched on the need to have 'specialists'. It is always worth asking if anyone else has been tackling this problem or has special skills that might lead them to expect to be involved. Even though they may not have succeeded in the past, they may be crucial to implementing the solution in the future so it can be worth engaging them regardless.

Psychological
Touched on above, there may be some people who should be

involved for 'psychological' reasons. It may be that their presence is necessary for the rest of the organization to 'buy in' – for example, a union representative might be included for this reason. Alternatively there may be a fear of certain groups 'sabotaging' a solution because they weren't represented – this seems to be common in some manufacturing processes.

Behavioural
Sometimes, we need to involve others, particularly in collecting information, when in practice they are unlikely to contribute anything new. For example, employee opinion surveys are often carried out with questionnaires distributed to every employee. The chances are that only a small percentage of employees really need to be asked in order to get a representative sample, but the whole group need to be involved so that they cannot say that they were not asked.

Senior management interference
It is often interesting for a group to see which senior managers take an interest in their work and which do not. The group needs to ask itself what the interests are that the person is serving – the company's, the group's or their own. If the first, then it is worth encouraging them but not heavily involving them; if the second, it might be worth keeping them closely involved; and if the latter, it is probably worth dissuading them sooner rather than later.

Vested interests (and hidden agendas)
On a similar theme, it isn't unusual for an individual with a vested interest to end up in a group. Although groups are generally quite resilient against such people, it is useful for everyone to be aware of the potential conflict that can arise. A common technique to resolve this, used in political subcommittees, is for each member round the table to make a brief introduction with three themes: their background and experience – why they are there, what they hope to achieve from participating, particularly if they are the representative of another group, and finally what might get in the way of their performing impartially.

There's no guarantee that this will expose all problems, but it will make people more aware of their responsibilities and the potential failings of their peers.

Conflict between individuals

Problems occur between individuals for a variety of reasons, though at the heart of most of these are some kind of misunderstanding, misinterpretation, or projection. Misunderstanding because I don't really hear the words that you said, misinterpretation because I don't see things the same way as you do, projection because I have experienced things differently in the past and am assuming that you are 'just the same as all the rest'. In this section we will look at some specific ways of improving our understanding of the dialogue between different people.

Non-verbal communication

Clearly, there is more to an event than just its superficial expression. When someone speaks they use different intonation, different expressions, choose words carefully (and sometimes are caught out by their unconscious substituting of similar words with a different meaning – the Freudian slip). In the following section we will look at the way in which we process this information and draw conclusions about it. Here though we want to see if there is even more that we can take in to help us subsequently interpret what is going on.

Many people regard non-verbal communication as a kind of pseudo-science. This is partly because they have only heard of a few hackneyed examples, such as people crossing their legs when they are sexually attracted (or repelled) by someone else. The other reason is that they have never properly observed themselves and looked at their own emotions and feelings when in certain postures or making different gestures.

The difficulty with non-verbal communication, or body language as it is more commonly described, is not observing it but interpreting it. You have to be careful not to draw inferences without evidence. The subject has been studied seriously since the eighteenth century and even Darwin published extensively on it. Because of the problems of interpretation and the importance of context, it has not progressed very far as a diagnostic tool. Probably the most comprehensive work in the area from a popular perspective has been carried out by Desmond Morris.[4]

To be an effective user of non-verbal communication you first need to build up your own powers of observation. As you begin to notice something happening, you can develop your experience of when it happens. This is similar to bird watching – people begin by spotting unusual birds and reaching for the guidebook to identify what they are seeing. Then they start to expect to see certain birds in certain places. As they become more observant they notice aspects of a bird's behaviour and can relate it to their experience of the bird and its relatives. When they spot a bird doing something unusual they are drawn to it, slowly developing an understanding of why the bird is behaving in this manner. So too with humans, except that you should have a head start because you are looking at your own species.

Activity 4.4

Here is a list of the common non-verbal actions that you will see in a work setting. Notice occasions when they happen, ask yourself in what circumstances they occurred and whether they repeat themselves elsewhere in the same circumstances. Try to envisage yourself in that situation – ask yourself what kind of gesture or posture you would be adopting and what you would be feeling or what your emotions would be doing. The more often you see something happening in a variety of settings but in the same circumstances, the more valid will be your assessment of its meaning. Ask yourself what your reaction (both verbal and non-verbal) would be to each action.

Smile	Pointing with a finger
Frown	Shrugging shoulders
Baring teeth	Thumb and forefinger making an 'O'
Open palms	Very firm handshake
Limp handshake	Hands in jacket pockets: thumbs outside the pockets
Thumbs up	Hands in jacket pockets: all hand in pocket
'V' sign – nails towards the giver	Playing with items of clothing (eg shirt cuff)
'V' sign – nails towards the recipient	Chin resting in palm
Hand over mouth	Chin stroked by palm

Lower lip between the forefinger and thumb	Fingers in mouth
Rubbing an eye	Chin rested on hand with fingers across the cheek
Rubbing both eyes	Chin rested on hand with first finger only on cheek
Scratching the neck	Arms folded; hands open
Pulling the collar	Arms folded: hands clenched
Rubbing the neck	One arm folded; other gripping it at the elbow
Rubbing the forehead	Standing with hands on hips
Rubbing hands	Sitting with hands gripping knees and bent forward
Rubbing nose	Sitting with one foot forward, bent forward and one hand on the upper leg
Hitting the forehead	Short gaze
Hitting the back of the neck	Long gaze
Clenched fist	Gaze with eye-to-eye contact often broken
Fingers in a steeple shape	Looking downward
Arms folded	Looking away
Rocking forward and backward	Hands behind back: open
Rocking from side to side	Hands behind back: clenched
	Hands behind back: arm gripped at elbow
	Hands behind back: forearm gripped

Case study 4.1

A manager in a health service department had acquired the habit of chewing the end of his spectacles when he was concentrating. He coupled this with a slight recline in his chair and an upward tilt to his head.

His department had seriously overspent its budget and his senior manager walked in to his office to discuss the latest excess with him. Unfortunately the senior did not interpret the actions as exhibiting concentration, but rather as a sign of indifference. Within a week the senior had reorganized the department and the junior had lost any influence that he had previously enjoyed. 'Trivial' matters like this can have a big impact.

ORJI Cycle

Behavioural scientists have a way of describing the thinking process that occurs in a meeting,[5] It repeats itself hundreds of times and has an enormous effect on how the meeting proceeds, how people feel at the end of a meeting, and what people think of each other. The most effective teams are those whose members are highly skilled at managing this process. Called the ORJI (Observation, Reaction, Judgement and Intervention) cycle, it is illustrated in Figure 4.5.

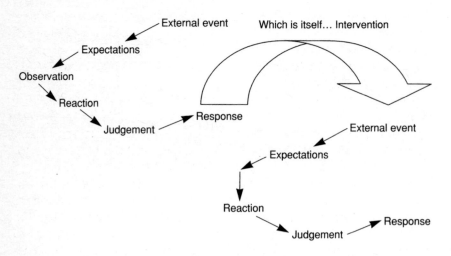

Figure 4.5   *The ORJI cycle*

Expectation

In the late 1970s there was a firm that produced politically sensitive signs and slogans. These were very popular with students at the time because they produced a shock reaction. Typical of the sort of message that they carried was, 'Thank God! She's black.'

People arrive at most meetings with preconceived ideas about what will happen and particularly about the people who are going to be there. For example, there may be one person whom everyone avoids bringing into the conversation because once started they believe that he or she will be hard to stop talking!

Observation

When something happens, people observe it using one of their senses. It is evident that if one of your senses is not very good you risk missing some events or some of the details about an event. If you find members of your group disagreeing with someone else, it is worth considering whether they had observed the information accurately. If not, you need to settle the dispute without making anyone feel stupid.

Reaction

When you see something happen you experience an immediate reaction. Your reaction depends on a host of previous experiences, particularly from the early years of your life, which form your expectations.

People with strong views have usually had many experiences that have tended to confirm their ideas. For example, someone who has a strong dislike of dentists will probably have had an unpleasant experience at the dentist in the past. Reactions are the basis of most prejudices.

Reactions cannot usually be controlled, they just happen. However, you can be aware of them and try to understand why you feel that way. On a longer-term basis, counselling can help someone understand why he or she feels a particular way about an issue, and then decide whether to continue to do so or not.

When strong prejudices come out in meetings, it is tempting for other members to make a joke of them, usually out of embarrassment. Unfortunately, this is often the worst thing to do, especially if the subject of the prejudice is in the team. Of course, prejudices are not reserved for people. They are just as likely to occur in other areas. Many dogmatic statements have their foundation in prejudice.

Helping other people to explore and address difficult issues can be a tough process, and some professionals would say it should be left to their expertise. Unfortunately, few people have access to such skilled help. It is possible to try to recognize consistent reactions among our colleagues and use this knowledge to help them see things from a different viewpoint.

For instance, two partners in a firm had different views about strategies for borrowing. One was in favour of building the firm by borrowing money, the other was strongly opposed to borrowing of any kind. As a result, the business was not growing to the extent that the first wanted. The two began to argue about the wrong issue. With the help of a facilitator the second began to recognize that his concerns about borrowing of any kind stemmed from his parents' personal circumstances during his childhood, and could see that his reactions were different from those of his partner. Although they never resolved the difference, they did stop arguing about the wrong issue.

Reaction is essentially an internal process. When you react to something you may change position to improve your observation, but you do not say anything and you show no signs of emotion. For instance, someone overhearing a comment may react by turning his or her head to improve the chances of hearing some more, but will not raise an eyebrow or let out a gasp.

As you become skilled at observing people at work in teams, you will notice when someone has reacted in a way that seems important. Skilled facilitators will ask the question, 'How did people react to... ?' to test the significance of a particular situation. The first few times this happens it can be disconcerting, but people soon learn to avoid criticizing others and to talk about their own reactions.

Judgement

Seeing something and reacting to it still have no effect on the dialogue. Before you make a comment, or any other kind of intervention (such as raising your eyebrows), you have to decide to do so. This decision may be conscious or unconscious.

One characteristic of a person's personality is a tendency to make judgements. Confronted with the same situation, some people are more likely to take a stance than others and can be very dogmatic, especially on subjects that are contentious.

The pro-hunting/anti-hunting or the pro-abortion/anti-abortion lobbies are good examples of this. Supporters on either side of the fence should be capable of recognizing that the issue is one on which opinion is divided and that no matter how strongly they feel, there is probably someone who has an equal and opposite viewpoint. Nevertheless, anger begins to develop as the more judgemental members decide to express or demonstrate their views.

At the opposite extreme are people who are strongly pragmatic. They will not usually intervene in a situation, recognizing that they are very unlikely to influence the course of events.

Intervention
So the sequence of events has evolved in the following way:

- A member of the team says something.
- You hear it, you see his face as he says it, you feel the table shake as he thumps it while speaking.
- Your experience tells you that people who thump desks and go red in the face while shouting obscenities either have a strong opinion about something or are drunk!
- You make your judgement based on your experience of this person, whom you know is abstemious – and think, 'He's on his high horse again!'
- What do you do or say? If you have thought through the implications of the ORJI cycle, have tried to understand your own reactions to the person, and have tried to see where misperceptions could have crept in, then what you say should have a positive effect.

The effect of your intervention will be to create another ORJI cycle in the people around you, and so the process continues.

Conflicts
This may sound like a rather tortuous process, but once you get the hang of it you'll find all kinds of dynamics going on in groups that you were never aware of let alone able to direct. You might be surprised how easy it is to resolve conflicts between two people in this way. Once you begin to recognize your own preconditioning and prejudices and seek to achieve positive outcomes without repressing negative stuff, you'll become a very valuable asset in the organization.

Transactional Analysis

Like so many of the techniques and skills in this book, analysing what people are saying is something that comes with experience. But unless you start somewhere you will never make any progress. One technique which is useful for understanding problems between people in meetings is known as Transactional Analysis, because it is used to analyze the transactions between two people. Eric Berne's original book on the subject was published in 1972, and this popular work has been reprinted almost every year since.[6] TA, as it is usually known, is based on some very simple ideas, such as 'I'm OK, you're OK', which you may already have come across.

First, TA recognizes that most dialogues are just that: someone stimulates the conversation with a sentence and someone else responds with a further sentence.

Second, everyone has three 'ego' states, that is, three different ways of thinking and feeling about yourself and the world around you. These three states are child, adult and parent. The child state (C) is how you used to react as a small child, usually concentrating on what 'I want' or being very compliant. The adult state (A) is very objective and looks coolly, almost computer-like, at the world around it. The parent stage (P) is based on how you were treated by your parents, or any other people that had a strong influence when you were a small child, and is probably how you treat your children if you have any.

To illustrate how the analysis can be used, in a simple conversation in a team meeting two individuals would probably begin with an Adult to Adult comment (AA), such as, 'What were the production figures last week?' said in an even tone. The response could also be Adult to Adult, 'They weren't as good as the week before'. This script would be described as AA–AA.

Alternatively, the response could be, 'You know perfectly well what they were!' This is the parent speaking, but to an adult not to a child so the script would be described as AA–PA.

Another alternative would be for the child ego to have spoken as if to a parent, 'Why do you keep getting at me?' So the script would be described as AA–CP.

It is easy to see that this is a useful way of describing what people are saying. It is particularly interesting if a conversation becomes emotive or if the group comes from very different backgrounds. The process of structural analysis allows you to see why particular pairs of individuals are irritating to each other.

To represent the different conversations a shorthand has developed consisting of three circles one above the other to represent a person and the three ego states. A second set of circles represents the second person. Lines are drawn to show the direction and type of comment.

Essentially the conversation will proceed effectively while the lines of dialogue, stimulus and response, are parallel. When they start to cross over, problems tend to arise. Although there are 72 possible crossed transactions, only four are common and these are shown in Figure 4.6. Work through them and you will begin to see how the diagrams and the conversations are working.

Activity 4.5

Now the fun starts! Using a video recorder, record a two- or three-minute fragment of a scene from a soap opera, preferably one with some heated conversation. Play back the clip a few times, identifying where the characters are placing the emphasis in their words and which words they use. Try to map the conversation using the symbols that have been described. Once you have mastered the process, record a different fragment, say from a play about business people. Repeat the mapping. Now if you are feeling bold, take a tape recorder into a meeting at work. Once you are out of the meeting play the tape back to a point where there is a lively debate. Map again. As you do this you will be greatly improving your skills of observation and analysis.

Activity 4.6

Review the section on the ORJI cycle. Remind yourself about the importance of timing your interventions. Now review the section about external experts. Imagine that you are sitting in a team meeting and can see that two people are becoming annoyed with each other. How are you going to handle this? Force yourself to make some notes. Try thinking of a few other situations and plan how you might handle them – concentrate especially on the four crossed ORJI transactions.

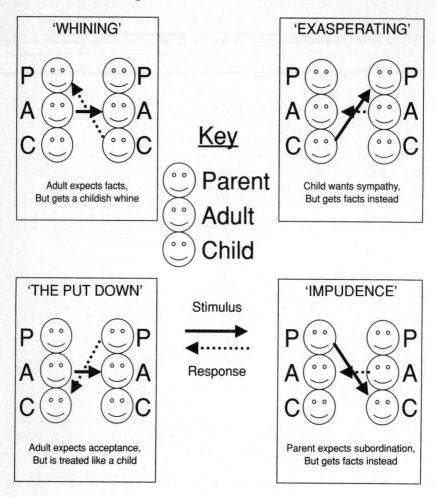

Figure 4.6   *The four commonest crossed transactions in TA*

Resistance

Now seems a useful moment to flag a further 'people' problem. Frequently teams encounter resistance to their efforts. This may take the form of starving them of resources, time, equipment, people or money but other forms of resistance are just as likely. For example, 'vital' information can be discovered after a study is completed and the results are presented, or perhaps the report disappears behind closed doors and the route that it has taken cannot be traced.

There are many good books on selling techniques and on consultancy skills. Most of these include suggestions about how to spot resistance and how to deal with it. It is well worth the group studying these as part of the problem-solving process.[7, 8]

MANAGING TEAMS

Decision-making

There will be many occasions during the life of a group tackling a problem when a decision has to be taken. There are several ways of arriving at a decision and it's useful to be aware of them. The commonest is probably the majority vote. It is quick and can give the impression that the group has made real progress. Of course, the reality is rarely that simple. Think what happens in a political debate. The majority might win, but the minority don't exactly swap sides – they just wait for something to go wrong and then say 'told you so!'. If the decision is fairly trivial and won't seriously affect the outcome of the team's work, then majority votes may be useful. If you need the full commitment of the group then it's better to try a different method.

Another common approach is the assumed close that is so beloved of salespeople and sometimes known as the consensus of silence. Here the proposer usually asks a closed question that needs only a yes/no answer, such as, 'Does anyone have any objections?' Most people do not like to break the silence and object because they fear being embarrassed if they haven't understood properly. Alternatively they could simply be bored or be desperate for a break.

It is difficult to think of a situation where the assumed close is a valid approach. It can in fact be a relief to people when there has been a long debate and there is no real conclusion. The co-ordinator may say, 'Would anyone object if we left this and came back to it another time?' You may even hear a spontaneous round of applause!

The third method of decision-making is well known. It is based on shouting down any objectors and is popular with people who have particularly loud voices. Unfortunately, these people are often also highly opinionated and the combination of the two characteristics presents a challenge for even the most seasoned team leaders. A third characteristic, which can result in an impossible combination, is if the person concerned is also in a position of power or influence. Frankly, the group might as well go home if this happens!

There are of course a few times when a decision is made unanimously. This is the fourth style of decision-making and can be achieved by any of the above methods.

A fifth approach is to adopt a compromise, usually the option of the least resistance or the most common denominator. It can be appropriate if the decision is a minor one.

The sixth and final method is the most appropriate if the group is not unanimous on an issue. It is called consensus. For some reason some cynics associate consensus with anarchy. They assume that it means that everyone has to debate and discuss and feel 'warm' and all sorts of other 'soft' things. It is, they say, not the stuff of 'real' managers.

Consensus decision-making is very different from the above description. It requires a ground rule to have been agreed in advance that says, 'We agree that all decisions will be made from the point of view of the team/department/company, etc and not from an individual's position.' This means that not everyone will wholly agree, but they will at least accept the consensus decision. Then when it is time to make a decision the question is phrased as, 'From the company's viewpoint what do we think?' or the equivalent. This removes most of the emotional concerns that hinder decisions and aligns everyone's thinking.

Structured approach?

In the following chapters we look at different ways of tackling problems, some structured and some not. If the group does decide to tackle something in a structured way then it is a sensible move for the stages in the model they are using to be summarized on a wall chart or similar device and displayed where they meet.

Physical environment

Today, the vast majority of group-based attempts to solve a problem still happen in one place. This isn't the only approach, but it is fascinating how we still haven't come to terms with working across telecomm links with videoconferencing and individuals in remote locations. Of course there are exceptions. For years there have been 'radio doctors' in Australia and astronauts millions of miles from their control centres. Today technology is slowly making in-roads. The present generation of laptop computers now has built-in cameras that can be used to capture images and transmit them via the Internet. In the North Sea, rig workers can carry a small camera around a piece of engineering equipment relaying the images back to a team of engineers in Aberdeen and London simultaneously. While they do so, the engineers make drawings on a special white-board and they appear at the same time on screens around the world. The computer program used to write this book allows mind maps to be created and notes appended and, via the Internet, enables the same images to appear anywhere else in the world. The technology is enabling, but it seems the resistance is in the human mind.

Meanwhile, back in the factory, our group might be faced with more mundane, but none the less significant issues. They need a room with sufficient light, heating and air circulation. The noise levels outside should not distract nor should too many interruptions be possible. The team will work better if it is not directly observed from outside through 'glass walls'. If the meeting room is too far away from the workplace, some people may feel uncomfortable and the travelling arrangements become more interesting than the problem itself!

The tables in the room should be arranged so that people are not intimidated by them, but can participate fully. A horseshoe is good if there is a speaker or if the leader is going to be presenting most of the time; a circle if the team is going to have an open discussion. Obviously people should be able to see and hear one another without twisting. If the team is to work all day, make sure that the chairs are comfortable.

Flip-charts provide a permanent record of the group's deliberations and so they are usually better than a whiteboard or chalkboard though today printing whiteboards are available and can be used to provide everyone with an instant copy of a complex chart or diagram. There are also whiteboards that can be coupled to a PC and can use optical character recognition to transcribe the notes.

Toilets, drinks and food arrangements need to be clear, and all the members should be told when major breaks are scheduled so that they can make arrangements for messages.

Ground rules

Although most group norms will only develop over time, it is useful for the group to decide on any issues that they feel are appropriate before they start in earnest on their problem. For example, the policy regarding smoking needs to be considered. More and more companies now have no smoking policies, but if not the group needs to decide whether it will be allowed.

Once agreed, these rules can be written on a flip-chart and pinned up at each meeting. Among the items could be guidelines on interrupting, asking if anything is unclear, sending apologies if people are going to be absent, topics that are taboo, and agreements about the ways in which the team will solve problems and make decisions.

If they are to meet for a prolonged time, it is useful to review the ground rules occasionally to reinforce them and to provide people with an opportunity to raise any new items or challenge any previous ones. This can sound a little false, but it is surprising the number of times that I have been asked in to help a faltering group and simply reviewing their *modus operandi* has allowed many issues to be raised and resolved.

Group members must respect the fact that everyone has the right to an opinion and to express it. Inevitably there will be some people who are less inclined to share their views. It is not the exclusive role of the co-ordinator to 'drag it out of them'. Every member has a responsibility to do so and it is a good idea to reinforce this in the ground rules.

If the group is to meet for a long time, some companies will provide training on how to be a team member. At least some of this will revolve around 'active listening'. If people are to be effective members they must be able to pay attention to their colleagues and listen to what they have to say.

In particularly traumatic moments the presence of someone else may be all that a person needs. However, being there or attending is not as easy as it sounds. Gerard Egan explains why listening is so important:

> Good listeners think more broadly – because they hear and under-
> stand more facts and points of view. They make better innovators.
> Because listeners look at problems with fresh eyes, and combine what
> they learn in more unlikely ways, they are apt to hit upon truly

startling ideas. Ultimately, good listeners attune themselves more closely to where the world is going – and the products, talents, and techniques it needs to get there.[9]

So listening skills are particularly useful to acquire, but being an effective listener is not as easy as it sounds. Some of the reasons for poor listening are:

- not being able to wait to say what you are thinking;
- being busy preparing your reply;
- evaluating what is being said;
- making judgements about what is being said;
- making judgements about the person that is talking;
- being busy sorting out your own preferences;
- finding that something already said has triggered your thoughts in a different direction.

If you want to listen effectively you need to listen actively. Active listening has three aspects: calming your mind; not being judgemental; and making sure that you have grasped the point.

Calming your mind

If you look at the reasons for poor listening, you will see that in most cases the listener's mind is busy on his or her own thought processes instead of paying attention to what is being said.

Not being judgemental

If you as the listener are judging the person speaking or evaluating what has been said, it means that you are not paying attention.

Making sure that you have grasped the point

Once the speaker has finished, try paraphrasing what they have said to make sure that your interpretation is the one that they wished to communicate.

NOTES

1   Maslow, A (1954) *Motivation and Personality*, Harper, New York

2   Johnson, D W *et al* (1980) Effects of co-operation, competition and individualistic goal structures on achievement: a meta-analysis, *Psychological Bulletin*, **89**, pp 47–62

3   Van Zelst, R H (1952) Validation of a sociometric regrouping procedure, *Journal of Abnormal and Social Psychology*, **47**, pp 299–301

4   Morris, D (1977) *Manwatching*, Jonathan Cape, London

5   Schein, E H (1988) *Process Consulting* (two vols), Addison-Wesley, Wokingham

6   Berne, E (1975) *What Do You Say After You Say Hello?*, Corgi (Transworld), London

7   Block, P (1999) *Flawless Consulting*, 2nd edn, Jossey-Bass, San Francisco

8   Whiting, P (1978) *The Five Great Rules of Selling*, Dale Carnegie & Associates, New York

9   Egan, G (1985) *The Skilled Helper*, Brooks Cole, Monterey

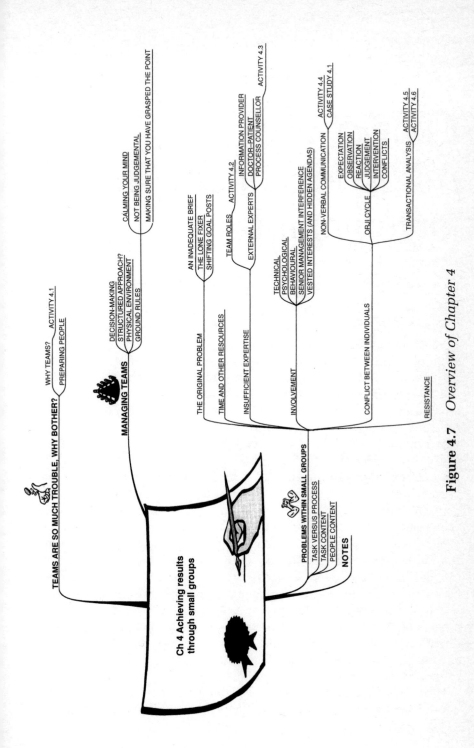

Figure 4.7 *Overview of Chapter 4*

CHAPTER 5

Conflict and misunderstanding in large groups

All too often in recent years, there have been major conflicts within organizations that have spilt out onto the rest of society. We have already mentioned the problems of Taylorism. Today, we see racial tension in German factories and similar unrest in Kent, nail bombs in the London suburbs of Brixton and Soho, claims of police harassment in Wiltshire as travellers try to get to Stonehenge, tunnellers being evicted from subterranean chambers on ancient woodlands, the tenuous peace in Ireland, violence erupting in French ports as British lorries try to enter and exit, the June 18 'carnival' in the City of London, and many other examples of wholesale confrontation or conflict. Conflict, of course, needn't be violent and so we ought to mention the empty housing estates in the North East of England, Canadian bans on blood donation by citizens who have travelled to the British Isles and the shareholder action activities in recent years connected with BP, Shell, ICI, and the building societies. Violent or not, the issues underlying are about major disparity across parts of society, some of it overt and fairly obvious in its origin and some of it very definitely covert and/or far from clear where it originated from. And we haven't even mentioned Kosovo and Serbia!

What has this to do with a book on problem solving? Well, I could have avoided the subject entirely and said that it was outside the scope of regular continuous improvement and so on. Of course the book wouldn't have been about problem solving then; it would have only been about continuous improvement. Behind many of the situations described above there is significant institutional involvement. This book is intended for people in institutions, so it would be short-changing you not to discuss this kind of problem. This is also a situation that is going to become increasingly significant in the future. Large organizations, particularly commercial ones, are increasingly pushing up against society's boundaries – challenging the way things are and threatening the stability that some people feel should exist. In recent months in the United Kingdom, we have seen the newspapers pushing up against boundaries of the law around privacy especially of public figures. Over the last couple of years there have been the proceedings in the United States between the government and Microsoft. One scenario of world futures early in 2000, created by a very credible think-tank in the United States, suggested that commercial organizations will play a predominant role in managing world affairs, including policing conflict and managing the differences between groups around the world. So dealing with conflict and misunderstanding in large groups is already, and will increasingly be, part of the role of people within institutions – people like you and I.

Less than five years ago, you would rarely have heard of the concept of conflict in organizations, yet today there are already many of us who are labelled as 'conflict resolution' facilitators. The significance of this field is growing and as it does so a few individuals begin to stand out. Among them is Dr Arny Mindell, whose approach of 'process oriented psychology' is increasingly drawn on. I hope that you'll be sufficiently interested to read more about this emerging role and so have included a reference to one of Arny's books later.[1]

COMMON THEMES

The following are just a selection of the commonest themes present in large group conflicts.

Perceptions of rank

Many conflicts seem to have an undercurrent of rank within them.

We use the term 'rank' deliberately because it is less value-laden than words like power, authority, and majority though 'rank' is still not the perfect term and perhaps someone reading this will feel able to share their ideas on a better one.

Rank is all around us. Large parts of our society are structured around a hierarchy with fewer people at the top of the pyramid than at the base. This may have evolved for a number of reasons but it is by no means the only way of organizing things and it is open to widespread misinterpretation. It is these misinterpretations that often create the seeds of a conflict.

While there will always be individuals who seek to exert power over others by virtue of their own perception of their importance, this isn't always the case. Senior managers may not consider themselves to be members of an elite within a company, they may feel that they treat their colleagues with equality and fairness throughout. But it could be that others don't see it that way at all. I brought a PC from a medium-sized computer retail company a couple of months ago. It hadn't worked properly from day one and I struggled for weeks to get them to fix it. In desperation I rang and asked to be put through to the MD. The switchboard wouldn't do so and even refused to tell me his name. In the United Kingdom, this information has to be made available so it didn't take me long to get his name from another source. But why were they protecting him so fiercely? Somewhere in the organization someone had decided that the MD shouldn't be exposed to upset customers. In today's competitive world it seems extraordinary that anyone should take such a step but, of course, it wasn't the MD that did so, it was others around him. He possibly sees himself as a most approachable soul yet it is his staff that have put him in a position of 'rank'.

It sometimes takes a joke or an aside remark to see the way in which rank is misinterpreted. A friend is a serving police constable, albeit nearing retirement. A while back he met the chief constable. In the brief social exchange that followed, my friend made the simple observation that the two men had something in common. The chief constable was intrigued – my friend explained that neither of them would ever be promoted!

Often people in positions of higher 'rank' do nothing to exploit it. It is those around them that do, who attribute to them powers that are way beyond reasonable terms and create protective barriers, even quite aggressive ones, to prevent the individual with 'rank' from being harmed, influenced, dirtied or whatever.

Less so today, but in the past many professions have been accorded status in this way. Some, within those professions, have managed to shed themselves of this status as they feel it may even get in the way of them practising their speciality. For example, many doctors would now like to be considered a part of 'normal' society. Clergy, magistrates, solicitors, teachers, bank managers, and so on are all having their 'rank' challenged and being placed more squarely within the community that they serve rather than sitting on the edge.

When we speak in terms of individuals, the legitimacy of 'rank' is easy to challenge. But what about groups? Often the *majority* assumes some form of rank 'above' the *minority*. Unwittingly even, their behaviour is the most common and so people who belong to a different group and display different behaviour are seen as being of lower 'rank' rather than simply behaving in different ways. Management books are riddled with such problems and I'm sure that this one is no exception no matter how much I have tried to avoid them. For instance, structured problem solving is a behaviour more typical of white males brought up in a Western schooling system. By insisting that people adopt a systematic approach to problem solving we unwittingly exert rank on those that don't work this way. If you are struggling to see how such an insistence can be made, you might like to look at the 'competency' system in your organization and see whether there is any evidence that the behaviours extolled *actually* contribute to the performance of the individual in their job. Competency systems often mention 'adopts a structured approach to problems' as a core competency for managers. For almost every group that you can identify, it is possible to find issues of rank related to other groups.

Another simple example is in the way that we discuss legal issues. The English legal system has been copied by many of our former dominions. Yet a court in the Bahamas is very different to one in Macclesfield. The culture of the English is not to raise our voices, to present a logical argument based on sequential, deductive reasoning. The culture in other parts of the world is very different – the power of someone's argument might not be measured by their erudition but by their forcefulness. Their logic might not be deductive at all but subjective and circumstantial. I enjoyed a conversation once with a woman with a very highly qualified legal background from Sri Lanka. She made an observation about someone who had just been imprisoned for a relatively small misdemeanour: 'He may not have done this, but he was as corrupt as you can get and so deserved to be put away for something.' As far as she was concerned, public perception of guilt was potentially more important than the findings of a judiciary. Often we assume that, because the other group doesn't behave in the same way as we do, they are lesser mortals than we are. Many Britons would be shocked at the idea of passing a harsher sentence simply because the individual was popularly perceived as being corrupt and might well extrapolate this to some lack of civilization in Sri Lanka.

An HR manager confronted by a rather noisy member of the workforce in a factory in the Midlands, came out with the statement: 'I won't discuss this with you until you conduct yourself in a civilized manner.' The person she addressed was the spokesperson for a group of workers from a different ethnic background. The result was nearly a full-scale walk-out. The message they had effectively received was: 'You are so ignorant and ill-educated that you conduct yourselves like farm animals and I would have to lower myself to talk to you.' An extreme example perhaps but it makes the point.

Even within seemingly the same culture there are subgroups whose behaviour isn't the same as that of the majority. For example, a disproportionately high number of senior managers are likely to be prosecuted for speeding and drunken driving. Their attitude is personified by the individual pulled up by police for driving up the hard shoulder during a traffic jam and unfortunately captured on video for posterity. Quite politely the officer explained to him that it was an offence to drive there and asked whether he had a reason for doing so. 'Don't you speak to me like that,' he replied. 'I'm a chartered accountant!' Again, the hidden message is one of rank: 'I'm better educated and superior to you *and* your laws.'

Over recent years, in the United Kingdom, a number of building societies have changed their status and become publicly traded banks. The usual outcome has been a moderate windfall for anyone with savings in the society (technically known as members). Not surprisingly those societies that have not made the transition have been under pressure from some of their investors to do so. The senior management of one such society recently embarked on the most extraordinary mail campaign to discredit an individual who had proposed that the transition should be voted on at the AGM. Their messages had little or nothing to do with the evidence for or against the transition, but instead focused on the lack of experience, narrow-mindedness, short-term outlook, and personal characteristics of the individual. Most of the 'members' looked on with some disbelief that their elected officers could dream of behaving in this manner. Again, the message was clear: 'Don't you dare tell us how to run this organization, you nasty little man!'

When we experience or witness major conflict between groups it is always worthwhile asking ourselves whether there is an issue of rank at play. Rather than being sucked into the debate either side, we can only draw on our own wisdom and try to resolve it openly.

Different experiences of the same events

Given that there are countless groups and subgroups within society, it is not surprising that a lot of conflict arises because of one group failing to see things from the other's perspective. Mediation, for groups as much as for individuals, is about helping the two groups to see things from each other's point of view.

The subsidiary of a large shipping company was experiencing a dramatic downturn in their traditional business and yet an increasingly demanding performance was expected by their parent company. The management team decided to reorganize and to refocus sales effort on alternative markets. It was a bold strategy and called for a big commitment, but they were adamant that they didn't want to make anyone redundant. Within a few days of the management meeting at which this was discussed, there was a report in the local press that speculated about lay-offs. That day the staff demanded a meeting. The chief executive gave a 'state-of-the-nation' address describing what had been agreed and how they were going to be calling on the staff for their support. The next day a delegation from the workforce presented an ultimatum calling for his dismissal and that of his fellow directors. The chairman stepped in and a team from the parent company arrived to review what was going wrong.

From the management team's perspective they had done a splendid job. They had devised a plan that would not only save the company but might even return better results than expected. They had already begun to see some success in the new markets and were confident that over a 12-month period they would have achieved an excellent transition. They were totally confused by the workforce representatives' reaction.

To the workforce the messages were far from positive. The company is not doing well. The people who got us into this mess have now decided to pursue new markets rather than put the mess right in the traditional ones. Even if they are successful, this will only guarantee them their jobs; the workers will probably no longer be needed and so will be made redundant while the company recruits others people with different skills. Survival of the company is of no consequence if we don't have a job!

The outcome of this conflict was the appointment of a new MD within a few weeks and a sideways move for the previous one. The new MD introduced a far more consultative style of working with the workforce, flattened the organization considerably and offered a voluntary retraining programme with fixed terms for people who took it up.

So often, tension is created between large groups because of a failure to see a situation from both points of view. A classic commercial example is the large customer's treatment of a smaller supplier. In the United Kingdom, the textile industry is in a state of near collapse. Foreign imports, of comparable quality yet made at lower cost because of lower labour rates, have undermined UK manufacturers to such an extent that they are folding under the pressure. They can do nothing to compete on labour rates so have to make their production processes far more efficient than elsewhere. There are limits to how quickly this can be achieved and yet the pressure is unceasing. The customer companies' staff are under pressure from their bosses to deliver to cost targets, and so the option of favouring local providers for a long-term benefit, for altruistic, for social, for political, or for humanistic reasons is simply not possible. It seems extraordinary, but one of the companies that appears to be single-handedly demolishing the industry, was extolled in the mid-1980s as an exemplar of modern management methods and customer focus. From their perspective they are doing the best they can for their customers. From their suppliers' perspective they are progressively and systematically putting them out of business. Such a situation is unlikely to be resolved unless the two bodies can somehow be brought together and helped to develop a mutually satisfactory solution; of course, to do so calls for extraordinary political savvy as it would be too easy for the situation to become one of a counter-competitive practice. This does illustrate again the power that large organizations increasingly have to influence and indeed control the world around them.

While it is easy to write about the problems of failing to see things from the other's perspective, it is a very different thing to do so. We are not merely saying 'see', we are actually calling for a depth of understanding that is difficult to achieve for ourselves, let alone for someone else's situation. However, it is only through this depth of perspective that progress can be made.

Inability to differentiate feelings

Feelings are difficult things! Not only do they sometimes seem to be painful, but they also seem to get in the way of a 'rational' solution. Hardly surprising then that as we grow up and go through life we evolve a myriad of ways of avoiding feelings as much as possible. Put two conflicting groups in a room and you'll often see only anger and adversarial behaviour. Ask the facilitators how they are feeling and they'll offer a wider range from fear, anger, numbness, disappointment, sadness, being overwhelmed, and so on. Most of us are unaware of our feelings in anything other than a superficial manner or under extreme provocation.

When we are confronted with a situation we react in ways that have become embedded in us from our previous experiences of being confronted. Of course, those situations may have been very different but our defences are not so good at discriminating between them and so adopt fairly static patterns.

I was working with a client company a little while ago. One of the managers was a fairly young person who had an extraordinary enthusiasm for his work. While his colleagues said that he wore his emotions on his sleeve they were only partly accurate. The closer you looked, you began to see that he wore only his positive emotions there. If something happened that excited him he was barely containable. In practice though, his negative responses were all held within; he was unconscious of them, and certainly no one got to see them. Despite his young age and relative fitness, he was on permanent medication for ulcers and suffered from a succession of minor infections and ailments.

Something early on in his life had taught him that he should always see life in a positive way and that the negative should be suppressed. This is not an uncommon pattern, though few people carry it quite so far. The result was an exceptionally motivating manager to be with, someone who could grab a new initiative and really make it fly!

However, put that individual into an environment of conflict and he would flounder. Like most of us he would find conflict intolerable – though in his case he would probably find it even more unbearable. None of us *likes* conflict but some of us can tolerate it more than others. If we are to do so though, we have to be very sensitive to our own feelings and where they are coming from.

Exploring our emotions is a personal inquiry – a journey that we can all benefit from undertaking. However, it might help if I was to share my own example to make the relevance clearer. I have to be very careful consciously to avoid taking sides, seeing things from both perspectives and helping the two groups to see things from each other's perspective. I say consciously because I know that I have a very strong sense of social injustice. I don't mean that I'm to be found at Speaker's Corner each Sunday or that I am a campaigner for Amnesty International but when I witness something it is the injustice of it that concerns me most. In working with groups, there may not be an issue of injustice in the conflict that we are working with, but I am almost preconditioned to see one and to side with the 'underdog' – even if there isn't one! This preconditioning stems from my early childhood and the relationship I had with my grandfather; it has served me well over the years but there are times when it is inappropriate and I have to be sensitive to this.

For most of us, insights to our responsive behaviour and sensitivity to feelings require a significant investment of time. Most people don't have this experience and so respond instinctively. The consequence is that many conflicts arise not because of direct confrontation but in both cases through conflict with other parties in the past.

A silly example might make sense of this. Batman is constantly in conflict with the Joker. There is no reason why they specifically should be in conflict. However, Batman's early experiences – his parents died tragically and he was brought up as an orphan – made him develop a profound sense of justice and in some ways his life could be described as trying to put right the wrong done to his parents and himself. This is not unusual. There are many people around who try to put right the wrongs done to their family by devoting themselves to a cause.

The Joker's life history is less well documented, but we can suspect some equally distressing family past. Somehow he is left with a similar sense of the injustice of life, though in his case he seeks not to right it but to contribute to it. This is also a common pattern, especially among late adolescents who find themselves in trouble with the law. In the Joker's case, we might also suspect that his defence of practical joking is a way of avoiding taking himself too seriously – presumably because to do so would be so painful as it would bring him into contact with the injustice that he suffered as a child.

So we are left with two individuals, whose responses to injustice were shaped a long time ago, who find themselves in conflict today. They are archetypes. Batman is the archetype for that part of each of us and of society that sees the world as unjust but capable of salvation if we all live our lives righteously. The Joker is the archetype for that part of society that bears a grudge for 'ills' long since gone and who seek retribution rather than reconciliation. Neither party can express its real anger about a specific set of circumstances in the past other than through conflict today.

The resolution of the Batman–Joker scenario is only going to be achieved if both groups can be helped to see what their real feelings beneath the anger are, where their feelings are really coming from and so discover ways of behaving in a less conflict-driven manner.

USEFUL ALTERNATIVE PERSPECTIVES

The first lesson in learning to deal with conflict in groups then is to be able to see things from the different perspectives of the many parties involved.

Seeing history the other way around

A few years ago I was very fortunate to be awarded a Churchill Fellowship that took me to Japan. While there I decided one day to visit the town of Hiroshima. I had no time to do any research and simply caught the first available train. Assuming that there would be some kind of memorial to signify the explosion of the nuclear bomb there, on arriving at the station I walked out into the spring sunshine looking for some signs. A nearby tram shelter indicated the Hiroshima Peace Museum and so I headed there. As you approach the museum you arrive on the opposite side of a large expanse of paving. Walking across it you see the remains of the twisted steel girders that once formed the frame of a large building.

If I recall the distance properly, it was some 300 metres above this that the bomb exploded. As you walk across the paving, individual Japanese students approach you inviting you to sign a peace pledge that you will do all that you can to discourage the use of such devastating devices again.

Entering the museum, you are taken on a tour of the local events immediately before the detonation, then see evidence of the destruction caused, hear eye-witness records of the event, and then learn of the aftermath. The bomb exploded during the 'rush hour' in the early morning. I shall never be able to forget the stones from the steps of a bank, where two people had been waiting for it to open. Their shadows were burnt into the stones by the heat and light from the explosion.

The peace museum makes no judgement other than to say that such power should never again be unleashed. It says nothing about the responsibility for the bomb; it doesn't mention the political issues at work, nor in much depth the historical legacy that led to Japan being at war in the first place.

With the exception of a handful of individuals, few of us are educated in more than one country. Our education inevitably draws on local versions of the 'truth'. Yet they are local versions. My school taught us European history from the period 1789 to 1945. The books were obviously English ones and they taught this history from an English perspective. At the very trusting age of 14 we were never led to believe that this was anything other than purely objective. We took on board the interpretation of events as if they were facts. It is too far away for me to recall the detail now, but I remember being surprised a little later when a German friend of mine pointed out some of the quite specific technicalities in these accounts that were not the same as the ones he had been taught. You might think that this sounds naïve but pause for a moment. If you didn't fall for this you are undoubtedly the exception. Most of us are completely unaware of the subjective nature of the information that we have absorbed over the years and this applies as much to science as to history or the arts.

History plays a crucial role in many large group conflicts. Often the only way to resolve them is for people to step back and be prepared to relearn their history from the perspective of the other group. I spent some time with a senior US union representative discussing the nature of labour organization in the United States.

His account of the history of industry was very different from the one I had heard elsewhere. He described the workforce of the late 1940s returning from war. They had been exposed to discipline and organization that many had never experienced before. They had returned with many lessons learnt. Concepts of rank were reinforced, where for many US citizens he felt there had been few before the war. The majority of servicemen had been of low rank and had their lives run for them by the military powers. They returned to a society where the more affluent had benefited from the war by investing in growing industries. The story went on. His account made it seem so reasonable that workers had to become collectively organized if they were to survive in this post-war economy. The account he gave explained why conflicts arose, clear rules for working together evolved, and a structure of national negotiation had been created. When I subsequently spoke to the vice-president of a major US manufacturing company his explanation of the history of the situation was completely different. Whether these two people will ever see eye-to-eye I have no way of knowing. However, for many groups the resolution of the conflict is for each to be given the space to tell the story of the past in their own terms, to be allowed to do so uninterrupted and with as open a mind on the part of the listeners as possible.

Frequently, the BBC has been lambasted for broadcasting plays and documentaries that explore the issues in Northern Ireland from the Republican perspective. In the long term, though, it has helped people to see life from just a slightly different perspective. The relevant history often goes back a very long way. It seems there is little point trying to negotiate a peace in Northern Ireland if we deny the history of the 1700s and even earlier.

Seeing history from the other group's perspective does not mean that we have to accept their subsequent behaviour but it does begin to allow us to understand that behaviour. It seems that often deep-rooted historical legacies lead to a predictable set of responses. Many of the world's religions sum this up. While they usually preach forgiveness and peace they also endorse revenge. They do not do so by chance. There is something in human nature that responds to abuse with a desire for revenge. When those that have been abused are in the majority (the mainstream) they often exert their revenge through the judicial system. When they are in the minority they often have little recourse than to act outside of the law.

The other collective response isn't entirely helpful either. If you go to a war torn area or to a city in which there is major industrial unrest you soon discover a large part of the population who will tell you that there is no problem. They act as though nothing untoward is happening. To the observer it is obvious that their behaviour is anything but natural; however, they will persist in their view that everything is 'alright'. Unless this group too can be persuaded to look a little differently, they simply preserve the environment in which the abuse is happening.

Seeing 'groups' the other way around

In any large group conflict there is likely to be one group that represents the 'mainstream' and one that represents the 'abused'. By no means do these always equate to majority and minority. They relate to positions of power and although they may be portrayed by each other as being right and wrong, good and evil, new and old, these distinctions too are unlikely to be accurate. To illustrate the impact of helping groups see things the other way round, I'd like to give an account of one such dispute that a colleague and I were involved in. I don't think that this was a particularly good way of tackling the problem and would be worried if anyone tried to copy it, but perhaps there's something for all of us to learn from it.

CASE STUDY 5.1

Two banks recently merged. Their IT departments became locked in conflict. Their systems were largely incompatible and this was reflected in the cooperation between the departments which was superficial at best. Massive investment in the past meant that both departments had extensive facilities and the prospect of relocating to a neutral new site was unrealistic. The 'battle' which this situation was rapidly escalating to assumed that one or other group would be closed down and the other would take over – to the best of our knowledge no decision of this kind had been taken, though there was a precedent in the branch networks of the banks where one group had already begun to be shut down. By virtue of the scale of the merger, one group was perceived as belonging to the mainstream and the other to the minority and the branch closures reinforced this. The inevitable assumption being made by the group members, but never actually articulated, was that the minority IT group would be the one that was also closed.

In the mixed group discussion that we facilitated, we began by helping people within the groups make explicit these fears and opinions. We stressed throughout that the pictures that emerged were their own and that there was no 'official' version being presented.

We then helped the groups put together a case for their own 'survival'. In order to do so convincingly they needed to understand the counter-arguments to their own proposal. Working in their groups they prepared the case. During the subsequent discussion the level of aggression and interruption was extraordinary for a 'business' meeting. My colleague and I sat through this. We only intervened when someone was completely prevented from speaking. People don't like anger when it is expressed. It is often very hard to remain quiet at such times. Our natural instinct is to try to step in and diffuse the situation. This happened often during the debates, and although we acknowledged the contributions made by the 'peacemakers', we did nothing to stop the flow of the dialogue. Probably three-quarters of the way through the meeting, the group reached a silence. The atmosphere in the room was tense, it was summer too which didn't help. There were a couple of directors present and they tried to get us to collude with them in relieving the tension. We sat it out. As you might expect, over the course of the day some unelected leaders had emerged in the debate. They had been the ones with the powerful arguments and powerful voices. After what seemed an eternity, one of them coughed and in a quiet voice, said: 'I think I may have been a bit silly here. It seems to me that there have been some interesting ideas put forward by some of us and while I've been arguing I haven't really thought about them.' He pointed to one of the people from the other group and added, 'You said something back then about changing how we have structured ourselves. Could you explain what you mean?'

The conversation took a completely different twist. In the next hour or so, the two groups explored their relative strengths, how they had been structured in the past and how neither had found this particularly good. They made suggestions about alternatives and began to acknowledge that each had some aspects that they were good at and each some that they were less effective at. By the end of the meeting a new structure was already crystallizing. In both cases it meant substantial reductions in overall responsibility and numbers of people, yet it honoured the contributions that they both felt could be made more of.

Seeing power the other way around

I've already mentioned the issue of 'rank'. I want to make a different point here about power and powerlessness. Again, I don't think that my own treatment of these issues should be seen as an exemplar, but it serves to illustrate them a little more.

There's a concept that people often mention about victims. The view is that some of us are 'life's victims'. These unfortunate souls are trapped into being victims because of their own mindset, which may have evolved for a variety of reasons but probably began when they were very young. The process of being a victim becomes a self-fulfilling prophecy. The more you are a victim, the more likely you are to experience subsequent events as a victim. Of course, the popular press will extrapolate this to whole groups and indeed I have often been led to believe by senior managers that their entire workforce have this 'victim' mindset. Therapists often report that there are some people who do have difficulty seeing things without a victim emerging somewhere along the line.

In a dispute, it sometimes seems as though one group has become the 'victim'. The role is an easy one for the media to project onto them too. These 'victims' respond in the ways we have described – either seeking to retain a strand of normality in their lives by denying that there is anything wrong, or by seeking revenge. By adopting this response they are reclaiming some of the power that it seems they have been robbed of.

But if taking up a stance of victim is a way of reclaiming power, what of the people in the other group? The mainstream group wishes to achieve something. They try to do so in a direct manner and it results in conflict. Rather than step back and try a different approach they engage in the conflict blaming the other group of being 'victims' and implying that they are the obstacle. The mainstream in this case are robbing themselves of power. They try to reclaim it by projecting the 'blame' onto the 'victims'. Neither group is achieving what they want. Both groups have ended up robbed of power and trying to reclaim it.

YOUR ROLE?

So you have decided to do what you can to help this large group with its problems. What should your role be? In the following paragraphs I have tried to summarize the differences between leader, facilitator, and elder. You might like to reflect on these and ask which you are being drawn towards. Are you comfortable with my definitions or would you amend them? Use them to define your

---

CASE STUDY 5.2

A steel company was struggling to survive in a complex, diminishing market with extraordinary price competition from foreign imports. They had to adopt radically different working practices and remove several tiers of management from their organization if they were to stand a chance of matching the prices of their European competitors. The workforce needed to take on board far more of the responsibility for the day-to-day operational activities without a supervisory structure. The company created a redundancy plan for the middle tiers of management and presented the workforce with the picture of the future that they felt was needed.

The managers were largely very happy with the plan. They stood to gain both immediately and in the longer term through the settlement. The stumbling block was the workforce. A nasty scene developed in which the employees downed tools and refused to undertake any new responsibilities. They claimed that this was yet another example of the management trying to get them to do more for less and they feared what would happen if anything went wrong – they expected people to be sacked.

After nearly three weeks of stalemate, the company directors were beginning to panic as they knew that the financial results were going to be grim and feared that the city would not support them as they tried to restructure the business.

Both groups had fallen into being victims, surrendered their own power, and were trying to reclaim it by blaming each other.

We were asked to intervene! How do you resolve such a situation? After some thought we decided to discuss the problem, as we saw it, with the two groups separately. We offered to do so with both groups and at first were only taken up by the management team who had after all called us in in the first place. Rather than address the issue directly we spent some time looking at the shifting balance of power and the response to adopt a victim stance. In the group and individually we looked at how this stance could be used as a defence.

---

role as you see it and if you are acting on someone else's instructions why not clarify their understanding with them before you embark?

Your motives?

A recurring theme through the early part of this book has been the fact that our experiences in our childhood influence our behaviour as adults. The influence can be conscious – as a child we may have enjoyed going to football matches with our father and as adults we continue this practice. The influence can be unconscious – it was only many years after I had passed my Class 1 advanced driving test that I realized that driving safety was something that had been very important to my grandfather and when I was a child probably the only thing that he had been obviously proud of was his driving record in the Post Office. Our lives are riddled with these connections. They affect us in relatively inconsequential ways like the ones I've mentioned but they also do so in more profound and sometimes sinister ones too.

Recently, the story of Kimberley May, the child who was switched as a baby in hospital and spent the first nine years of her life with the wrong parents, has come to light. As the papers said: 'In an ironic twist of fate, her own child has just been taken away from her, in much the same way that she was from both her genetic and adoptive parents.' That isn't a 'twist of fate'. It is a pattern repeating itself.

When people take on public office something is driving them. More often than not it is something from their past that is spurring them on. I've already given the archetypal examples of Batman and the Joker. What do you think might drive someone to want to be Prime Minister or President? In recent months, Hilary Clinton has described her husband's upbringing as unloving and used this to account for his infidelity.

A survey of Times 1000 senior managers showed that a startling and statistically significant number of them had been paternally deprived as children. As little boys (the vast majority of them are male) we learn two major lessons from our fathers. First, we learn that there is someone stronger than us out there. We absorb this into ourselves as a lesson that there are limits to our power. Second, we learn that our father is in a relationship with our mother that is unique to them as a pair. It is not a relationship that we can have with our mother. In time, hopefully, we will meet someone else and have a similar relationship with them but it won't be our mother. We absorb this as a lesson that there are some things out there that we can never have. Imagine that you have never learnt these lessons. Imagine that, as far as you are concerned, there is no limit to the power that you can wield and there is nothing that you cannot have. Sounds frightening if it is carried to excess perhaps, but in moderation what a combination if you are to become the head of a powerful corporation!

So you would like to be involved in resolving conflict amid a large group. Perhaps it's time to consider why. What is driving you? You need to reflect on this. Have you always felt that way or has something sparked it? If you know what has sparked it, are you confident that doing so will really serve your purpose? If it will, then are you confident that others will not suffer as a result?

To give a painful illustration, there are many charities that have been started up by parents immediately after the death of their child. The charity is often established to try to address the cause of the child's death. The energy behind the anguish that the grieving parents feel is diverted to raising money for the charity. Every individual is different, but we have to ask whether the parents have really grieved for their child or are deferring doing so. Even if they have, are they trying to absolve themselves of a blame that they have adopted for somehow not saving the child? The charity's cause may be laudable, but if the motives of those who establish it are not clear then there are dangers. The organization may not help the parents deal with their needs and they may at best lose interest or at worst break down with the unresolved distress. If it has been moderately successful in raising funds, what happens to the benefactors and their contributions? If it has raised the hopes of potential beneficiaries, what happens when these are dashed?

Perhaps the conflict that you are drawn to work on is in your company, community, family, society or wherever. What is drawing you to do so? What will you get out of doing so? Will everyone appreciate your intervention? Who will not? What will they think? Why? Are you really taking sides? Or will some people see it that way? I hope that this won't be the case but it's only by asking these questions that you'll discover the part of you that is being stirred up.

One final illustration may help put this in context. I was in a medical waiting room recently. The atmosphere in the room was intense. There was discomfort all around – it was quite palpable. The other people in there were clearly avoiding eye contact with anyone else. No one was smiling. You could have heard the proverbial pin drop. It seemed that all the appointments were to begin on the hour. As people were collected they shuffled off, glum, depressed even. When I had an opportunity I suggested to someone in authority there that this wasn't a very nice environment for people to be kept in and that by simply staggering the appointment times they could avoid it or at least minimize the discomfort people were feeling.

I was taken aback by the anger with which he spoke. 'What is it to you? Are you their self-appointed spokesman? Is there anything in life you won't try to control? If they want to change something then let them do so! You don't have to all the time!'

I'm still not comfortable about his reaction, but I can see the wisdom of his questions. Why did I feel I should intervene on their behalf? Perhaps they were 'happy' with the kind of atmosphere that pervaded in that waiting room. I will never know, but I do now question my motives with a renewed vigour when I am tempted to respond to an injustice as I perceive it.

Once you have considered your motives, the next step is often to review the role that you will be adopting.

The leader

It is sometimes quite easy to find ourselves in a role of leader. We may feel ill-equipped for it, but simply by taking the initiative when others don't puts us there. By doing so we are making a statement about ourselves – about how we stand on an issue, about our levels of tolerance, about our needs to be surrounded by others who feel similarly. The leader is in a powerful position but is lost without others who can follow. Adopting the leadership role places a lot of responsibility on us.

The facilitator

The facilitator is different from the leader. The facilitator is using certain skills and by becoming a facilitator we are saying that we believe, we hope, that our skills are up to dealing with the problem at hand. It implies that we believe we can work alongside the people who are trying to resolve the issue, that we shan't be seen to be biased or distorting the truth, that we can be trusted. If anything happens to destroy the trust that we are asking them to place in us, then our position is jeopardized at the very least. So we try to be as authentic as we can. We avoid behaviour that would create an impression of bias.

The facilitator's skills are in helping others to reach conclusions. They may be led to make a decision but should not be directed as to which solution to adopt. The solution will hopefully come from within them so that they feel a sense of ownership for it and therefore have greater commitment to make it work.

The elder

A word is emerging, based on the anthropologists' expression, for those people who will contribute to resolving the problems of large groups. The word is 'elder'. It is distinct from 'leader'. In many early communities, the tribes had both leaders and elders. The former took the tribe into war, or onto the plains to hunt for animals for food. The elders, on the other hand, resolved questions that arose in the community, settled contentions among the members of the tribe, and would engage in the peace-making after a battle.

Just as it is difficult to define what the skills and qualities of a leader are, so it is with those of an elder. The following is an attempt, but it is by no means comprehensive and certainly needs expanding on.

An elder is endowed with the trust that a facilitator strives to earn. The elder has often earned this trust a long time ago. While the elder is trusted, they may also be seen as biased – biased towards the status quo. This isn't always the case but it does happen. Though biased, the respect that they command balances this bias and those who work with them take it into account when deciding on their viewpoints. In a sense the elder is a facilitator with attitude! By being more overt about their views they are able to be more authentic, but at the same time they wish only to influence others to make a decision in a way that will make them feel comfortable rather than the elder.

Being in the spirit of the moment

Elders know that there are no rules or procedures that will force a resolution. What works one time may work another or it might not. They also know that no one is all good or all evil – so they are prepared to see the good in everyone and try to help others see it too. They are also careful to help those who might appear predominantly good see their faults too.

As they aren't bound by rules, precedents or 'sides' they can 'go with the flow'. They sense the moment and respond accordingly. If there is tension 'in the air' they sense it and live with it rather than unconsciously or consciously trying to quash it. Their spontaneity helps others bring the emotions of the moment into the conscious world.

Seeing things the other way round

We have already mentioned the importance of seeing things from the other group's perspective. This skill is well developed in the elder. They will constantly be trying to experience the world and events through the senses of the people they are working with. They will do so at the individual level, though bearing in mind the implications for groups and whole communities.

A kind of attitude

The attitude of the elder is not a 'holier than though' one. It is totally accepting of others without necessarily adopting the same thoughts and attitudes as the others. The elder doesn't act as judge of the others but instead helps the various parties to make their own judgements.

Even if the elder isn't involved in working with more than one group, they will still try to explore the impacts of the behaviour of one group on another. For example, one of my colleagues was working recently with a charity. They were unable to make progress on a new fundraising initiative because of some bureaucratic procedures that had to be gone through. It seemed at first that the delays were causing frustration internally and morale was slipping among the employees. She spent some time with the group talking about their work. After a while she speculated on what the founders would have thought about the new fundraising effort. She placed a large chair on the edge of the circle that the employees had formed and named it after one of the founders. By giving this unseen and forgotten 'hero' a presence in the meeting the group were able to engage in a one-sided dialogue about the charity. In doing so they could express their reservations about the way it had lost contact with its original ideals and methods. The loss of morale was more deep-rooted than had previously been thought and it seems likely that the 'bureaucratic delays' were some kind of unconscious projection by the employees.

Awareness of ourselves

As adults we have learnt to respond to different circumstances in different ways. The lessons will have been learnt in our childhood. For example, when we saw someone being picked on in the school cloakroom we may have felt anger, guilt, sadness, amusement, or one of a host of other emotions. Our emotional response then will have combined with our rational mind and we'll have decided how to express this emotion. Perhaps we ran away, joined in, cried, tried to stop the bullying or were just plain scared. If there was any discord in us, between our emotional response and the physical one, then we will have experienced that discord far more deeply in us. Today, when we experience something akin to the bullying but in a different context our reactions are strongly influenced by this earlier experience.

The elder is constantly trying to understand his or her own reactions, at the emotional level, to the events around them. These reactions may give insight into the feelings of others so they mustn't be ignored, but equally they may confuse the feelings around and need to be filtered out. This is a complex activity that calls for a lot of self-awareness on the elder's part.

Living with pain

Just as aspects of our lives will have been painful so will aspects of the conflict we are working with. The elder will have worked through their reactions to such pain. In this way they can offer a less subjective response. This is not easy. The vast majority of us, understandably, find it almost impossible to tolerate much pain. After all, that is the purpose of pain – it is the body's way of saying, 'Watch out, you are being hurt!'

In a large group setting, we often find ourselves struggling to prevent the peacemaker in us trying to stop the group from feeling this discomfort. Our defences simply kick in. Someone says something that we feel is nasty, provocative, deliberately going to incense someone else. The group takes a deep in-breath – often audibly. Someone, instinctively, tries to deflect the comment from its intended victim – often by means of humour. The group releases its anxiety by laughing. The moment passes.

The elder, on the other hand, often through presence rather than words, inhibits the peacemaker. The elder sits allowing the moment to grow rather than deflecting it. The elder encourages the speaker to elaborate and then the victim to describe the pain that they felt. This process can fall apart at any moment but the elder is comfortable with the pain and can hold it as often as need be and for as long as it takes.

NOTE

1   Mindell, A (1995) *Sitting in the Fire*, Lao Tse Press, Portland, Oregon

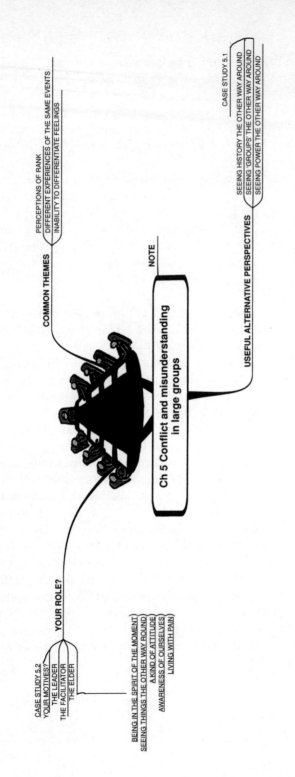

COMMON THEMES
PERCEPTIONS OF RANK
DIFFERENT EXPERIENCES OF THE SAME EVENTS
INABILITY TO DIFFERENTIATE FEELINGS

NOTE

Ch 5 Conflict and misunderstanding
in large groups

USEFUL ALTERNATIVE PERSPECTIVES
CASE STUDY 5.1
SEEING HISTORY THE OTHER WAY AROUND
SEEING 'GROUPS' THE OTHER WAY AROUND
SEEING POWER THE OTHER WAY AROUND

YOUR ROLE?
CASE STUDY 5.2
YOUR MOTIVES?
THE LEADER
THE FACILITATOR
THE ELDER

BEING IN THE SPIRIT OF THE MOMENT
SEEING THINGS THE OTHER WAY ROUND
A KIND OF ATTITUDE
AWARENESS OF OURSELVES
LIVING WITH PAIN

Figure 5.1 *Overview of Chapter 5*

CHAPTER 6

I can't change – can I?

It sometimes seems that we are being asked to take on board more and more change. It seems that just when we've got our minds around one way of doing something, we have to stop doing it that way and start doing so in another way. It's easy for all this to get on top of us and for us to begin to feel quite depressed by it. Of course, some people seem to adjust very easily. They just thrive on new ways of doing things: new structures; new processes; new procedures, and so on.

I remember spending some time with a manager in a large transport company. He bemoaned the changes that his firm had been through, the pressure placed on them from outside, the exacting demands now being introduced by their customers. He also described the majority of the other employees and their less-committed attitude. It seemed that many of his peers would come in to work on the dot of their contracted time, play football in the yard during their lunch-breaks, then go home on the dot of the designated finish time. He was often there for an hour longer in the evening and at least half an hour more in the morning. He felt he wasn't properly respected by the company and didn't get a fair increase in salary each year given his level of 'commitment'.

We explored a lot together but two things stood out. First, somewhere he was equating 'hours' with 'commitment'. Someone who spent an hour more on-site was more committed. His fear was that if he was anything less than totally committed (on his scale) he would be given the sack. Yet there were lots of others who didn't put in the time he did and they weren't sacked. So he built up resentment against them. When asked to change, or do something different, or come in for an exceptional job, and so on, they were always there. They were no less committed – they simply demon-strated it differently. He, on the other hand, found change annoying – he resented it. Resentment seemed to be getting in the way of change for him.

Then we tried an exercise together. I asked him to draw up a timeline. It looked at the changes he had experienced in his life from the time he was born to the present day. The pattern was extraordinary. From the age of three, when his parents had divorced, until he was 17, he had moved with his family eight times. He left home then, and moved a further three times in the next three years. From the age of 20 he had only moved twice and they were both times when he had been made redundant and had to go elsewhere to find a job. Resentment was his script. He used it to cope with anything that happened outside his control.

So we looked at all those moves. When we had finished he began to marvel at how he had coped with so much change. By the time he started work he almost had a PhD in handling change! No wonder he had eventually found somewhere that he could feel stable, though it was also not surprising that he felt threatened and quite insecure in his jobs.

If you have any doubt about your ability to change, if things around you seem threatening, it is often enlightening to look back and see whether you have coped with such events and pressures before.

Activity 6.1

Draw up a timeline for yourself. Start with a sheet of paper, at least A4 in size, and draw a diagonal line from one corner to the opposite one. Label the line with 0 at one end and the 10-year point older than you are now (if you are 37, mark it 40; if you are 52, mark it 60, and so on). Divide the line into equal 10-year stretches.

Now mark on any significant events. Show when you went to school, when you changed school, when you left school, any university dates. Add relationships – when they started and when they finished. Add jobs – when you started and when you left as well as any promotions that you got.

Put marks to show the birth of any children that you have or are special to you – such as nephews, nieces, grandchildren, godchildren, and so on. Also add marks for changes of home. By now you will have got the idea so just add marks for any other events that seem signifi-cant to you.

Spend some time just mulling over the diagram. Sleep on it and then add any more points that come to mind.
If you have started keeping a family history you might like to add this document to it – future generations will be very grateful!

PROBLEMS THAT WE CREATE OURSELVES

While a lot of problems around us, especially at work, may seem to be outside our control and largely caused by external factors, there are some problems that we create for ourselves. Ironically they are often more significant to us as individuals than almost any other. Certainly they are in the background of most changes of job.

Not being integrated

Have you ever noticed someone who never seemed to get disturbed by catastrophes as they happen around them? Someone who remains calm despite all kinds of problems and conflicts? They project an air of grace, of calmness, of maturity and balance?

For years management development trainers and HR professionals have struggled to define this quality of character. These individuals are few and far between, yet they strike you almost as soon as you meet them. These people inspire us with their quiet confidence and genuine nature. They don't engage in petty politics and they won't stoop to the smutty or stereotyping behaviour that underlies most forms of bias, bigotry or racial or sexual inequality.

You might expect them to have risen to the most senior positions in organizations. Certainly some have, but there are some cultures within organizations, even whole industries, that simply don't favour them, so they may well be behind the scenes in these. It seems that there is no clear pattern to the type of person that exhibits these 'Buddha'-like qualities. They may be male or female, old or surprisingly young, of every race and so on.

You might like to think about the people you know and see if there are any that would fit this description. They are not perfect, they are not gods, and the assessment is your own, but it might help if you can get one or two in your own mind.

There are lots of ways of describing the character, but not so many that can be used to explain it. One way of looking at these people is to say that they have accepted certain fundamental things about themselves, their lives and the society in which they live. Without becoming too academic, in a sense these are the fundamental truths of existentialism. You might like to explore this topic more as it also provides a good background to the difference between structured and unstructured problem solving which we describe in practical terms in Chapter 8. We can summarize the key themes that these people seem to have accepted.

1. *That while they may make some contribution to the world around them, they are nevertheless a very small cog in a very large wheel.* A huge amount of effort is expended in activities that the people doing it perceive is of enormous importance. In practice most work is self-justifying. Initiatives like business process re-engineering, total quality management and the high performance workplace have unearthed some of these practices, but they still predominate. There are still many people in work who fervently believe that they must put in 12-hour days and that the work they are doing is essential to the survival of the organization. Sadly, they are usually deceiving themselves.

2. *That everyone, including themselves, must eventually die.* Again, a lot of people put themselves under terrible stress, ironically because they are trying to put back the clock and pretend that they are not getting older and so closer to dying. Look at the advertisements in magazines and on television. How many of them are offering ways of pretending or denying that we are getting older! In recent years, men's 'lifestyle' magazines have taken off. They promote a lifestyle that is probably healthy and positive but the reasons many people buy the magazine are far from healthy. For most people the inevitability of death is something that they don't confront until they reach middle age, often when their own parents die. Only when we can accept this obvious fact, does our life potentially become more enriching and enjoyable.

3. *That, ultimately, we alone can make the decisions that affect our lives.* So much individual anxiety is brought about by assuming that someone else has done something that will hurt us. This is at the root of most office politics. It is behind the scenes in most commercial negotiations. It is embedded into our society in remarkable ways, such as adversarial judicial and political systems. It is the ultimate defence, against being hurt,

to blame someone or something else. So often, we hear the words 'they'. 'They' are demanding unreasonable pay terms. 'They' won't acknowledge that the work is far harder and more complex than ever before. 'They' keep throwing rubbish on the pavement. 'They' don't manage the roads like 'they' used to. 'They' means 'Not I' and that means that I am avoiding taking responsibility for this myself. Of course, we can't all fix the world's problems, but we can take responsibility for our own. If something terrible seems to keep happening at work, what are we doing about it?

4. *With choice comes responsibility and with that comes freedom to do as we feel is right.* If we don't like something then we have a choice – we can choose to put up with it or we can choose to do something about it. What we do is not dictated by anyone else. Our choice is our own. The people that we've described have a clear sense themselves of what is right and they live by that sense. It may not be the same as yours or mine, or even popular codes like those of most religions, but it is theirs. No one can force us to do something that contravenes our own code – they may try but we choose to go along with them. This is probably the worst kind of dilemma for many people. What do you do when you are told to do something at work that you think is wrong? You can refuse, but what will happen if you do? Will you be sacked? Will you be bullied? Fortunately, few of us are really forced into the situation of having to resign because of such a conflict though it does happen. More commonly, the sense of disquiet grows unconsciously to the point that we can take no more and so find another job.

While you may not entirely agree with this kind of interpretation it is useful to consider these 'lessons'. If an individual hasn't accepted them, they are going to burn the midnight oil, they are going to be frustrated, even angry, with life, the system, and people around them. They won't enjoy their work though they may put up with it.

Not being engaged

A second source of enormous frustration at work, which then percolates out in conflict, is where an individual is 'simply' not engaged in the work that they are doing. What do we mean by 'engaged'? There's a world of difference between people who go to work because they enjoy what they are doing and those who simply sell their time to an employer. It doesn't matter what you do or what the job is, you can take pride in it, you can despise it, or you can merely do it.

I live and work in Central London. Each morning, I walk across Regent's Park and down Marylebone High Street to my office. At the end of the High Street there's a nasty road junction with cars coming from several directions. There's a pedestrian crossing there. During school terms, for three years now, there's been a young man wearing the distinctive cap and yellow jacket of a School Crossing Patrol. He is impeccably turned out. He smiles at parents and children alike. He times his holding of the traffic perfectly – judging when to stop a vehicle and when to keep the children waiting. I know nothing of his background, why he does this job – part-time and in term times only. I guess that one day he'll do something else. What I do know is that he has made an indelible mark in the local community. He will be long remembered by the children and parents he has helped and by other passers-by who, like myself, can't help but be touched by the engagement that he has for his work.

Sometimes we have to ask ourselves why we do the work we do. If it causes us so much anxiety, so much frustration, so much loss of sleep, isn't it time to say 'enough is enough' and find something we can really engage in?

Needing someone to engage us

Of course, it's all very well saying that we should be 'engaged', and also that we alone can take responsibility for our lives, but it certainly helps if we have others around us who appreciate and nurture us. At home we need our partners, friends, family and children to provide this kind of support. Without them we become lonely, lose our self-respect and sense of judgement and can find trivial things getting out of perspective. At work, we need the support of colleagues, our manager and others in much the same way. Again, without them we lose our own sense of contribution, of self-worth and perspective.

Sadly, a lot of problems happen in organizations where the management style is driven by a need to deliver precise results and the way that this is achieved is by disregarding the human needs.

Ironically there have been countless studies that show that people who are nurtured deliver greater results, yet still the response to a pressure to deliver, in many organizations, is to apply pressure on others negatively.

In any organization where there is a sense of stress, where there is evidence of a workforce buckling – high absenteeism, high sickness levels, rapid turnover – it is worth looking at the management behaviour.

A SENSE OF PURPOSE

The first step to changing is to begin to gain a sense of our own purpose. If you haven't already done so, go back to Chapter 2 and review the activities that you did there. If you didn't do them then, please have a go now, it will make the next few sections far more real for you.

We all have a sense of purpose

We do all have some sense of purpose. Often it isn't explicit, but it is always there. It may take some effort to acknowledge it but it's generally worth the effort in the long run. If you have done the activities in Chapter 2 you should have begun to see some of the patterns and drivers in your life so far. Try summarizing these now in bullet points or on a mind map.

This chapter is going to call for some quiet reflection. You might want to save it for a quiet time on your own, or you might know somewhere that will be the right time to give it uninterrupted space.

Activity 6.2

Spend a few minutes thinking about yourself at work, in your present role. What is it like? Do you enjoy it? What particularly excites you and what frustrates you? Try to feel those emotions as you think about the role. Try to see yourself as you are working with others. What kind of relationship do you have? What kind of role is it that you perform? Be honest with yourself. Now consider what you are bringing to the workplace. What 'gift' are you making to the people there? What is the impact that you are having? Don't excuse yourself by thinking of it as insignificant or negative – there must be a seed of a positive contribution.

CASE STUDY 6.1

Anna was a 17-year-old who worked in a well-known service company a little while back. She was the office junior and mail-room clerk. When you caught sight of her she rarely had a smile and you might have wondered what she got out of being there or what her contribution was. When you asked her what she was going to do at the weekend it usually revolved around going out with mates and 'just hanging about'. In fact she was a perpetual hanger-about. She hung about at work and she hung about at home. It was as if she was constantly waiting; waiting for something to happen that she needed to be there for. It turned out that this was a pattern set up early in her life under very sad circumstances, and it seemed as though she was destined to repeat it for a long time to come. When the organization decided to streamline some of its activities and reduce costs she was one of the people who was asked to leave. It seemed that the company didn't have a need for someone to just 'hang around'.

It was some years later that I learnt what she had gone on to do. She had joined the armed forces, spent three years there and then left and become a fire fighter. Apparently it's a role that she has taken to fabulously and has been constantly promoted and praised for her bravery. She has, it seems, discovered her sense of purpose. It may not remain the same for all her life, but right now she is very satisfied.

You may not be able to answer this question right now, but allow your mind to wander. Ask yourself what you might be doing if this were a perfect world and you could do whatever you liked.

The difference between essence and personality

There is a school of psychotherapy, known as psychosynthesis, which draws on other sources too, that suggests that we might have two dimensions to us. The first is personality and this wraps around the second, essence[1]. The personality is shaped by the world around us. It is our defences. In the case of Anna, just mentioned, her 'hanging around' was a way of coping that she had to learn as a small girl. She had immense patience, didn't expect anyone or anything to amuse her while she waited. She could simply hang around for long periods of time. While she drew on this patience in her earlier role, it wasn't until she joined the fire service that she seemed to find her essence and at this point her adult life took off. Some people might suggest that she was still playing to her defences but the passion that she felt towards her new role suggests that there was something deeper.

For some of us the real essence seems to be evoked in our lives outside work. We may make pragmatic choices to remain in a well-paid job rather than turning a lifelong passion into a new career. Of course, it's fine to make a pragmatic choice provided that beneath it there isn't a ferment of resentment, anger, disappointment and loss of self-respect. For many there comes a time when the compromise is no longer acceptable and a change will happen. There are countless examples of people in successful careers who reach their middle age and consciously choose to change direction. While many of these involve a 'down-scaling' in income, seniority, prestige, international travel or whatever, there are also many that work the other way round.

Perhaps it is time to consider your colleagues and friends? How many of them (and look closely at their partners too) have made such transitions or are in the process of doing so? In their efforts to create a learning culture within them, a few companies have introduced a system whereby employees can choose the subject that they study in their allocated training time. Often the topics chosen are quite enlightening. One organization had people taking up musical instruments in their middle age; young people studying for GCSE O and A levels that they had always wanted to take but the curriculum hadn't allowed it at school; several staff taking Open University or part-time degrees; sports coaching and adult teaching qualifications featured quite often too. These are not necessarily people who have discovered some true sense of themselves but the likelihood is that they are on a journey along which they may do so.

Discovering our true purpose

So we have spent quite a lot of time examining this sense of purpose, looking at how failing to give it sufficient attention can create problems at work and, of course, at home. Although I have given some examples of people who have found their purpose and got in touch with the essence rather than their defensive personalities, it would be wrong to give the impression that this is an easy or a quick process.

Working on finding a sense of purpose is a long process and it is one that seems to make most leaps forward when we are not working on it at all. The key, however, is to be prepared to challenge ourselves, slowly beginning to recognize our emotions, and asking ourselves where they come from. Separating out feelings that are our own from those that others project onto us or we project onto them, we begin to see that life is not as simple as we perhaps thought it was.

Eventually our patience is rewarded and we begin to see the light, as it were. But it isn't easy to give up what we already have – not just the physical things but the emotional too. We become very attached to our defences and it is very difficult to step clear from them. Now that we have begun to see that it is possible in many ways to change, the next chapter looks at why it is so difficult to do so!

NOTE

1   Schechter, H (1995) *Rekindling the Spirit in Work*, Barrytown Ltd, New York

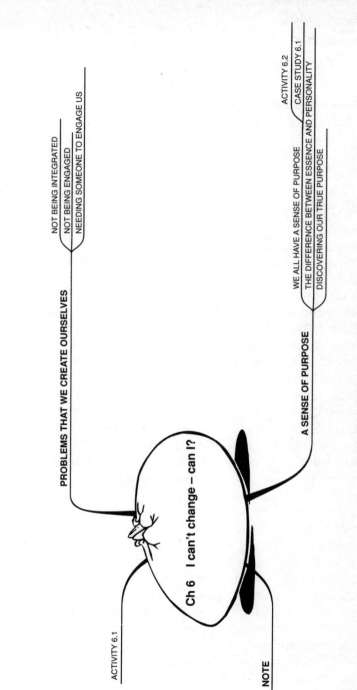

Figure 6.1 *Overview of Chapter 6*

CHAPTER 7

Transitions

Although this chapter is in the middle of the book, it was the last one I wrote. For weeks, I put off writing it and would find all sorts of reasons for not even starting. In the last three months, I have had three computers break down on me. Each has had to go to the repairers and in one case it wasn't even capable of being patched up. Each time was a great excuse not to get on with the book – you'd be amazed how much time I can spend loading up my software onto the replacement machine, configuring it all perfectly, recreating templates and macros, etc, etc. Being in the middle of the book meant that any neat, structured way of writing sequentially through the book was blocked, so for months I have deferred writing almost anything – it took a great force of will to complete the subsequent chapters – and still this one eluded me.

Last night, I finished formatting the text and printing it out ready to send to the publisher. I spent yesterday doing the illustrations and checking the references. Still I hadn't started this chapter. As I walked home in the early hours of the morning I asked myself, what was going on? Why had I let this simple chapter hold me up for so long? As I strode, my mind began to float off into that meditative state, the runner's high; the chapter took shape; my key themes emerged, even a few sentences and paragraphs evolved.

As I neared home, the question came back to mind – why was I having so much difficulty getting this chapter written? A word that is increasingly entering into popular usage in the English language is 'synchronicity'. It was coined by Jung to describe how remarkable coincidences can occur in our lives. How often I have heard people say that they were called into their manager's office on a Friday and told that they were redundant, only to have a telephone call 'out of the blue' from an old friend wanting them to consider joining them in their new business.

Some might say it was ironic. The chapter is about making transitions happen and the key in so many instances is about letting go of something. Of course, what I was doing was holding onto my project, my 'baby', for as long as I could.

FEELING THE DISCOMFORT

It is important to stress how, even when the present is intolerable, and the promise of the future is so wonderful, people still find it so tough letting go of what they know and are familiar with. I have very little experience of domestic violence, but I am led to believe that this is one of the contributing factors why some people remain in a terrifying, cruel, environment for so long. Certainly, it is one of the reasons why people remain in relationships that have long since died and hold little or no joy.

We often 'know' that something needs to change. We might acknowledge that emotionally too it would be better – there would be less frustration, less anger, less disruption, less distress, less whatever. Yet even that isn't sufficient. It sometimes seems that our language gets in the way. 'Emotions' have become modern currency. In his book, *Emotional Intelligence* (1996),[1] the journalist Philip Goleman tries to convey a sense of spiritual awareness in terms that business people will understand and accept. Ironically, if you read many of the accounts of the subject that have appeared elsewhere, the message has been lost completely and those very business people have struggled to put the concept in terms that they can understand, namely, structured, logical, rational, measurable ones. Today, you can even buy a 'psychometric' instrument that it is claimed can measure 'EQ'. Even the term 'emotion' has a rational air to it.

What stops us from moving on, and stops people in organizations from moving on, is not lack of knowledge, nor is it 'emotional non-engagement' as I heard someone say recently! It is at a gut level – they simply find it too painful.

I attended a wedding a little while ago. The bride's father was a very well-known industrialist, a man highly regarded by the City for his ruthless handling of ailing businesses. I walked outside the reception marquee in the early evening and, strolling through the garden, found him leaning back against a wall. He was shaking and at first I thought he was unwell but soon realized that he was crying. The pain of the loss of his daughter, as he saw it that day, was so powerful that it had penetrated even his extraordinary defences.

Feelings as a block to change

If the word 'pain' sounds like psychotherapy speak, I make no apologies. Most of us have invested enormous amounts of energy in building up our ability to tolerate pain. Pain is not just caused by physical conditions. It is also caused by mental and emotional ones and our defences against these sources of pain are complex and extraordinarily effective.

Whether it is a mechanism itself or the result of a highly effective set of defences, feeling no pain at all must be the ultimate protection. So often people say they are 'fine', act as if nothing is bothering them, and deny any kind of feeling about things that are happening around them. By reading this book, you are taking a stance – as somehow leading people through change of some sort. If you are going to ask them to do so, it seems only fair that you too are prepared to explore some of the discomfort yourself.

Activity 7.1

Find somewhere quiet and safe to reflect in. Think back over your life and try to recall a few significant events; perhaps at work, perhaps at home. Maybe people or animals you were close to who died; perhaps events in your education, family, love life. Allow yourself to sink into the feelings that you have around the event. Perhaps you were exuberantly happy, perhaps you were desperately sad and cried. Allow those feelings to surge around you. If you find it hard to remember how you felt or to experience the feelings then acknowledge it – this is exactly what we are talking about.

Now try something the other way round. When was the last time you cried? When was the last time you felt uncontrollably furious with someone or some organization? When was the last time you felt totally let down and disappointed? When was the last time you felt totally free from worries because you were so happy? When was the last time you felt immense pride at something you had done? When was the last time you felt immense pride at something someone else had done? When was the last time you felt that glow of warmth as a friend or partner comforted you?

If you haven't been drained by this process then it is worth revisiting and revisiting. Until we can really get in touch with how we are feeling, how can we possibly lead others through such tough experiences?

The (in)ability to experience fear

I have deliberately focused on feelings because so many of us have difficulty really identifying with them and recognizing when we are experiencing them. The tension that is behind them is one of fear. As we resolve problems at work, we frequently find that the most irrational things seem to happen to obstruct the process. Strategy changes; immediate events prevent long-term actions; key players are seconded to remote locations, and so on. While a lot of these can be imagined and somehow planned for, they too are often examples of ways in which we are unconsciously avoiding doing something different.

It fascinates me how we have created a society in which it is so hard for people to admit that they are frightened. Fear is something that we experience because of the 'unknown'. We don't know how the world outside us is going to react to something and so we don't do it. There are thousands of examples of fear-based inertia.

Have you ever attended a meeting where everyone knows something is wrong but no one will dare to say something? It doesn't matter how clever the facilitator is, or how tangible the issue is, people won't talk about it. Then, when someone eventually steps across that threshold of the unknown and does say something, it is as if the floodgates have been opened. I was asked to observe the management meeting of a company recently where sales were plummeting, costs were accelerating out of the roof, the bankers were refusing payments from accounts and a financial nightmare was unfolding. The team spent nearly an hour on the early part of the agenda, including discussing the staff Christmas party (it was June!), before someone eventually had the nerve to say that they felt it might be more constructive to talk about the real problems. Worse! It was me who said it!

EXPERIENCING OURSELVES DIFFERENTLY

Hopefully, as you read this book, and work through some of the activities, you will begin to see a little more of your own reactions to events and think about them. The key to much problem solving is helping people do things differently and to do so they often have to experience themselves differently. If we want employees to take responsibility for problem solving on the shop floor, for example, they don't just have to learn a kit bag of new tricks. They have to unlearn the stuff that tells them they are no good at solving problems – baggage that they probably acquired a long time ago – certainly before they joined your company. Then they have to see themselves as potentially being able to do things they never thought they could do. And eventually, as their confidence builds, they will begin to experience themselves in a different light and so take on responsibility for solving problems on their own.

Again, in a moment of reflection, you might ask yourself when you have experienced yourself differently. For example, in my own life, I know that I am now a very different person to the one you would have met a few years ago. A lot has changed around me and there has been no one single cause of that change, but I can begin to see the difference.

A few months ago, I was working with some fire and rescue service recruits. They were put through some extraordinarily tough activities and harrowing experiences in their training to prepare them for the work they were about to do. One evening, talking to some of them, one individual said, 'You know the thing that amazes me is how much I have changed in the last three weeks.' He went on to explain how his attitude to life had changed, how much less stressed he was, how much less angry he was, how his wife was glowing when she saw him whereas before there had been a growing tension between them. We do all change through time, but it isn't always that easy to experience it for ourselves.

ADDICTION

Everyone has heard of workaholism. The workaholic is addicted to work. Work is just the same as a drug (including alcohol). It forms a habit. It provides structure to our lives – we get up at a certain time, we travel to work in a certain way, we do things at work in a certain way, and so on. We soon get to a point where we can't cope with ourselves if we don't get a fix of our substance – in our case, work. But what is it in work that makes it so addictive?

All addictive substances enable us to escape from reality and so escape from (especially) negative feelings. Eventually we find that by having them they allow us to survive. If you have never seen an addict experiencing withdrawal then it is worth having a look around you next time you go on holiday. Check out the hotel lobby on the third day of the holiday. Watch those telephone kiosks and see who goes to make a long-distance call away from their room. Or go to the newsagent and listen to the anxiety in the voice of the middle-aged business man (or woman) who is losing their patience with the Spanish-speaking shopkeeper because the flight didn't bring sufficient English language papers this morning. Then ask the barman which day is the busiest in the week at lunchtime.

Begin to see work as it is – an addictive substance that we are hooked on and that enables us to avoid the pain of our feelings. Then you begin to see why it is so difficult getting people to accept change in what they are doing.

THE VOICE OVER OUR SHOULDER

Habits form early. If work is addictive, then it should be recognized more widely as such – but it isn't. Hard work is lauded in our society. And as if hard work wasn't enough, in the 1980s we were being asked to work hard *and* play hard too. In job interviews people even proudly declare that they have a strong work ethic. What does this mean? It means that the addiction they have was created very early in life.

Some people are so addicted that even though they realize that their health is suffering they can't stop themselves working harder and harder, longer and longer, less constructively and less constructively. They 'know' that they will be a better contributor, and will achieve far more by working less, but they just can't stop.

When they do eventually accept that they need help kicking the habit, they will sometimes acknowledge the voice that is constantly present over their shoulder. They can even have quite lucid conversations with it – how it is telling them to keep at it, to just do another half hour, to just finish this report today so that tomorrow is easier, and so on.

Do you have a voice over your shoulder? Try having a conversation with it. Try inviting someone else to look over the other shoulder and have the opposite discussion. It is probably these arguments that you will need to use with the people who are resisting the solution that your team have developed or are creating the problem that you are trying to resolve.

THE VALUE OF HONESTY

With so much denial going on at work it isn't surprising that most people find it extremely difficult to be honest at work. One senior manager explained to me that he couldn't be honest at work, because it was his job to motivate people and if they knew what he did they wouldn't work as hard. He was serious.

One facilitator draws on a North American Indian tool. It is a speaking pole. The pole lies on the floor in the room. If someone holds it they can speak openly, honestly, and impervious from attack by others in the room. It takes a bit of getting used to but soon people report that the tool has enabled them to speak openly and honestly in their workplace for the first time – no longer fearful of the reactions of their peers.

Spend a few moments asking yourself just how honest people are in your organization and how this might be influencing their perceptions of what you are trying to do. While it is easy to wrap up honesty as a component in the communication mix, it is often more helpful to acknowledge it as a problem in its own right. You can spend a fortune on 'good communication' and get nowhere because people are still avoiding being honest. Today we even have a word to legitimize dishonesty – it is called 'spin-doctoring'. The interesting thing is that it is the doctoring that gives it away as a bad thing, so now many people are dropping the last word and instead talk of putting a different 'spin' on something.

FEELING GOOD BY BLAMING OTHERS

Of course, every child will tell you that it is blameless and will project their blame onto others. It is another habit that we often carry to work with us. We wouldn't be in this mess if our customers/suppliers/the government did... !

By blaming other people we avoid feeling guilty ourselves. This hardly needs any further expansion. Stop it yourself and challenge those that use it with you.

FEELING GOOD BY BEING BLAMED BY OTHERS

A wonderful twist on blaming others is to blame ourselves. This is the abused's paradox. They perceive it as their fault that they were abused. Just as we would try to challenge this mindset and encourage them to see things differently, so we can challenge those who blame themselves inappropriately at work. Try to spot some examples of self-blaming at work. You soon find them. People will preface their conversation with 'I'm sorry... ' or 'Forgive me for... '.

We blame ourselves because our sense of self-worth is low. When we have a greater sense of self-esteem we no longer blame ourselves for things and we take the initiative to resolve them. Why is this significant here? If you are trying to sell an idea or solution to others and they are not adopting it, try asking yourself why. If the culture is based on people who have limited self-worth, then they are unlikely to adopt your solution wholeheartedly. Your problem is not one of selling it to them, but far more extensively to do something to raise their self-esteem and shift the culture.

WHEN THE TIME IS RIGHT

Sometimes, even the best solution doesn't sell, no matter how good the design, marketing and selling. Pity the poor fellow who invents the perfect way of humanely ridding a house of spiders but does so early in winter when there are far fewer spiders around. Sometimes, even the best ideas have to wait for the time to be right. While there might be some things that you can do to change the timescales around you it is often important to live with this and wait for the right moment.

Symbols

One glimmer of hope while you are waiting can be to look for symbols that tell you that you are right and that your time is coming.

CASE STUDY 7.1

At one of the major clearing banks, a small group of employees was trying to address a particularly difficult procedural issue. They had made formal presentations and all kinds of informal ones but nobody with authority seemed to want to do anything about it.

One morning, one of the team was talking over coffee about a dream she had the previous night. Nothing exceptional but it was a memorable dream for her. One of her male colleagues commented that such conversations had never taken place before. They spent a few minutes reflecting on how many things seemed to be changing in what was and wasn't acceptable at the bank. That afternoon, there was a meeting that happened to be attended by a more senior executive manager. Quite unconsciously one of the team started speaking: 'I know that in the past it hasn't been acceptable to raise this issue, but I wonder if we could look at... '. The procedure was discussed, the executive took it on board, and today it is commonplace throughout the bank.

NOTE

1   Goleman, P (1996) *Emotional Intelligence*, Bloomsbury, London

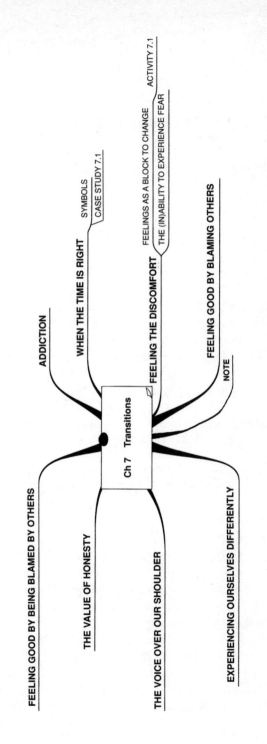

Figure 7.1 Overview of Chapter 7

CHAPTER 8

Unstructured problem solving

This might seem a contradiction in terms to some people. How can we possibly write about unstructured problem solving in a book? That might be an intellectual argument but there are some serious facets behind it. The fact remains that more problems are resolved in an unstructured manner than in a structured way, yet I have come across no other management book that dares to address this. Perhaps we are becoming more aware of the possibility and will begin to see more emerge. If this book appears in a further edition, perhaps this is the area that will grow.

IS THERE A 'RIGHT' WAY?

For some time now, management texts have referred to the work of Sperry (1996)[1] and others that illustrated that the different hemispheres of the brain were responsible for different things. In the fairly basic model, the left side is responsible for structured thinking, linear concepts such as language structure and algebra, while the right side works on patterns and geometry, takes a holistic view and links seemingly unconnected themes.

It doesn't seem too far-fetched to suggest that it might be useful to be able to try to call on both sides either together or individually in our attempts to tackle a problem. After all, what have we got to lose? Despite this acknowledgement that there are at least two ways of looking at a problem, approaches that try to emphasize the 'right' side tend to be ignored by mainstream management development. Those that do are often hybrids, for example, Tony Buzan's mind mapping which is just as structured as a piece of linear prose although it draws heavily on pattern recognition and geometry.

In the Middle Ages, one test used to detect witches was to throw them something and see which hand they caught it with. If it was the left (Latin *sinister*), then they were burned, if it was the right (Latin *dexter*), they were simply dexterous and released. Then people were quite prepared to accept the wisdom of this approach. Today we take a more clinical approach. From split brain surgery of severe epileptics, where the *corpus callosum* which joins the two halves of the brain is cut through, we know that it is the right side of the brain that largely controls the left hand and vice versa. No supernatural explanation is needed when we have a medical one! In some cases the behaviour that attracted attention to the suspected 'witch' was also probably due to this dominance of the right hand side of the brain. For instance, someone who was highly perceptive about others could well be picking up visual clues from their face. These clues are sufficiently subtle that most of us would not pick them up. The nerves from the eyes cross over through what is known as the optic chiasma. Thus images from the left eye are received by the right side of the brain. We now know that judgement of emotions on a face is driven more by information from the left eye than the right, so an individual whose right hemisphere is 'predominant' will be more receptive to such things than another. Again, no supernatural explanation is needed when we have a medical one! But hold on just a moment. The distinction isn't always so clear.

It is worth pausing for a few moments to ask yourself what is going on when you hear someone say certain things at work. For example, I overheard a group of consultants raucously laughing at a particular client company, a major and very well-known UK plc, because they postponed a meeting so that their clairvoyant could visit them with his observations on next year's product range. The consultants derided the company for being so stupid as to rely on a clairvoyant rather than market intelligence and scientifically derived consumer surveys. It is the society norms that dictate our response to many such situations. In the consultants' society, clairvoyants were not to be taken seriously, whereas in the company's they were at least as credible as market research (and also a lot cheaper!). The company had the advantage that they had used the same person for several years and experience told them that the advice they received was valuable. What would your reaction be?

A radio presenter recently poked fun at a local firm that had had its offices visited by a Feng Shui master. Yet the company had obviously believed sufficiently in the importance of the advice that they would receive. Who do you believe? The 'scientist' or the other person?

Many of the ways in which we look at human behaviour and personality derive from Freud, who began in exactly this way; with a physiological explanation that progressively evolved into less testable, but for many people, more satisfactory explanations (Osborne, 1993).[2] These alternatives continue today and exist alongside one another. For example, the treatment of schizophrenics combines medication for disease of the dopamine pathways in the brain, with psychotherapeutic support for what are suspected to have been intolerable personal circumstances that their condition enables them to cope with.

Notwithstanding the companies mentioned above, our commercial society tends to censor approaches that are unstructured and lack 'scientific' method. In post-war years a similar censorship has evolved around religion. Relatively few people will bring their religious persuasions to work and allow them to dictate how they work or take decisions. In the earlier part of the 20th century this would have been far less likely; indeed, many well-known firms were proactive in their support of religions, especially the Quaker movement. Nowadays, there have been a number of cases where people of other races have insisted on practising their own religious beliefs at work and have been discriminated against. It is also worth remembering that there is a substantial and growing New Age movement that perceives things very differently too.

All of this preamble is intended to make us stop and think. The next time we feel obliged to respond in a linear, logical and structured fashion, it is worth asking if this is really the only option or could we instead try something different.

It may not seem easy at first, we might feel a little odd but then we felt that way when we first learnt to ride a bicycle and sooner or later we got the hang of it.

THE UNCONSCIOUS

People don't usually have difficulty accepting that there is something called the 'unconscious'. What they do have difficulty with is understanding when it is acting and how to interpret it, let alone use it. By definition, the unconscious is something that we are not conscious of, so it is a little difficult to be aware of it. What we can do is be aware of ways in which the unconscious affects us. Perhaps the closest many of us come to experiencing the unconscious is on a car journey. We have been driving for some time, probably on a motorway, when we suddenly realize that we haven't been aware of where we were for some miles. Everything has happened safely, we have been travelling where we wanted to go and so on, but we simply weren't aware of it. It is as if our surroundings had ceased to exist for a while. One long-distance swimmer reported the same phenomenon – after a while her body had got into a rhythm, she was swimming perfectly well and was fully awake, but somehow she was oblivious to her surroundings. I don't pretend to be a great runner, but even I can go out for a run and find that I'm suddenly aware of having missed a few hundred yards or maybe a mile or two. In each of these cases our conscious has somehow made way for the unconscious. We don't know what the unconscious was doing, although it seems to have kept us out of trouble! With practice it is possible to switch into the unconscious state. This is what happens in meditation, which we shall pick up later.

When this happens to me while I'm running I'm aware immediately afterwards of a sense of having been floating. I suspect that anyone watching me wouldn't have noticed a thing, but for me there was a period when I felt I was really running effortlessly. This may sound strange, but I've read enough accounts of others experiencing similar sensations to know that it is a common phenomenon.

If it happens while I'm driving I often find that beforehand I had been thinking over some 'big issue' but on coming back into the conscious state I have formed some kind of plan to tackle it. For example, I might be wondering how I am going to write a proposal or structure a speech. In each case I'll emerge with a plan of what I'm going to do. It has obviously been a creative process that has been going on even if I didn't know it at the time.

These states are similar to the sense of daydreaming. They also seem to happen when we are passing from sleep to awake and vice versa. Many people say that they have their most inspiring thoughts when they are in the bath. With the heat of the water and perhaps already tired, they lapse into that half-asleep half-awake state and their unconscious somehow takes over. While I'm not a walking zombie when I get up in the morning, I also find that a warm shower first thing can produce a similar response in me. I'll cease to be aware of time passing but will suddenly find myself turning off the shower with a clear plan of campaign for the day ahead and perhaps even a letter or two mentally written.

Betty Edwards, in her excellent book, *Drawing on the Right Side of the Brain* (1993),[3] describes this state as the way in which an artist sees when they are creating an image, as she puts it, a 'drawing mode' of consciousness.

So what is the brain doing while we are in this altered state? Freud proposed a very simple mechanism for the behaviour of the mind at these times. Essentially, two forces are acting in the unconscious at any time. The first is concerned with pleasure. It is this that would like to be expressed and is linked with almost anything creative and pleasurable, particularly with being free from anxiety, which in classic Freudian theory is sexual in its origin. But all kinds of factors have told us that it isn't acceptable to seek pleasure in these ways, so there's a second force, the reality principle, which keeps the pleasure-seeking dimension repressed. It is the conflict between the pleasure and the reality principles that cause us so much mental anguish and it is the failure of the repressive process that can be experienced as being particularly creative. Of course, being creative isn't always nice but that's another story!

So we have something called the unconscious, that can be experienced at almost any time, and that can emerge when it isn't being sufficiently repressed. It seems that it is tied up with being creative and leading to the solution of problems. Can we then use it to tackle problems in the same way that we might use a structured approach? Well, the beginnings of the answer to that question can be found when we see what happens when we dream.

TAPPING INTO SOMETHING DIFFERENT

Dreams

As we have said earlier, many of the problems that we encounter at work are to do with relationships. They reflect a conflict of some kind between different people. It is often difficult to see for ourselves why they have arisen, why there is a problem in the first place, and how to resolve it.

Dreams have great potential as problem solvers, especially in situations like this. Again, we can turn to Freud who believed that all dreams are significant and worthwhile examining and interpreting. Dreams, he said, are always meaningful. Every dream has a cause, whose origin is in the repressed pleasure-seeking dimension. Unfortunately, we don't remember this underlying cause, only the ways in which it appeared in the dream which is why dreams need to be interpreted. Freud felt that the material of the dreams comes from three different sources: recent events and emotional situations; a blend of different sources; or an important event being represented by a recent unimportant memory.

According to Freud, the purpose that dreams serve is to relieve us of the tension created by a wish that we have but have forbidden ourselves to acknowledge and so repressed. Let me give an example. I found myself constantly treading carefully around a particular individual at work whom I didn't trust. I had no grounds to confront them as there was never anything tangible that they had done, but I was simply uncomfortable when dealing with them. After a particularly difficult day, I went home and had a restless night. At some point I woke up and realized that I had been dreaming. In my dream I was sitting in a restaurant when a large bird sitting at an adjacent table collapsed to the ground with its foot trapped in a can. I am terrified and wake up. I am terrible at recalling dreams or thoughts that I have at night so I keep a pad and pencil beside the bed. I quickly jotted down the dream and promptly fell asleep again. The next morning I woke and saw the pad. As I was late for work I didn't do anything with it and left it there. But the dream was still with me when I got to work so I mentioned it to a colleague. With her help, I remembered a time when I was a teenager when I had come across a seagull with its foot trapped in a can. Despite the gull's violent response, a friend and I managed to gather it in a coat and he held it while I removed the can and cleaned up the wounded leg. We released the bird which stood still for several minutes looking at us before very gracefully flying off. As we thought about this, I became sure that the large bird represented the colleague who was a very tall woman. I began to wonder if her behaviour at work was being caused by some metaphorical can that she was trapped in. I resolved to suggest that we had lunch together. In the course of this she shared a lot of the pain that she was feeling. While the situation was never properly resolved, life became a lot more tolerable for myself and some of my other colleagues and this particular person began to do something to address some of her issues.

Dreams are not difficult to interpret if you remember a few basics that Freud originally identified. First, in dreams one image can represent several things. Just as the bird in mine represented the gull and the colleague, I suspect it also represented other people who have been trapped and who I have worked with or who have been members of my family. Second, feelings connected to one thing are displaced onto another. In the conscious world I was so angry with and frightened by this woman that I found it very difficult to feel any compassion towards her, no matter how much I would have liked to and felt I should. In my dream, though, I could feel compassion for the bird although I was terrified by it. Dreams are visual and sometimes the images are so powerful it is difficult to see their connection to the 'story', but this usually means that the story is powerful too and worth pursuing. In dreams, symbols are particularly important. The can in my dream is not only a trap but also a container and while I was releasing the bird I was also providing a replacement container for my colleague's feelings. While she was trapped her feelings were contained in her emotion and attitude to others but if the trap was released she needed someone to help her contain them. Finally, Freud warned that once you are awake a dream can be elaborated on in such a way that you aren't aware that you are moving further from the story rather than closer to it.

Problems at work can be very creatively resolved through dreams. Try to capture your own and perhaps even be prepared to share them with others. You might be surprised how many of your colleagues have similar experiences and it can be good fun to try to explore them together. Freud reckoned that the things that led to a dream almost always happened the day immediately before, so the old adage of tackling a problem by sleeping on it is well founded.

Activity 8.1

You may prefer to record the following script on a dictation machine and replay it to yourself so that you can listen with your eyes closed, or you may find that you can work through it yourself by reading it. Of course you could also ask a partner or friend to read through it for you.

You are standing on a cliff top. Look behind you and see the green fields and the rolling hills. Feel the wind in your face blowing over the fields and over the cliff. Feel it flapping your clothes. Turn forwards and explore your clothes. What are you wearing? Look at them as they flap and see their shape, their cut, their texture.

The wind is getting stronger. You feel your arms lifting and as they do so your clothes billow out. At first it is slow but then faster and faster, you feel yourself leaning forwards and the wind lifts you. You sweep gracefully over the cliff and upwards. You are soaring, soaring over the sea. You look down and see the waves swirling and the shore disappearing behind you.

You look ahead and see a misty cloud. It is cotton-like; soft and warm. You feel yourself carried into the cloud. The mist is all around you. It feels warm and comfortable. You find yourself drifting into a sleep.

As you wake you are still in the cloud. The sunlight is intense and the cloud is bright. You see it thinning out ahead of you and the blue sky is just visible through the haze. In the distance is land. You see the shoreline. Can you see people? They are down there. What are they doing? What kind of country is this? Do you think they are of our age or from another time? Like an eagle in the hot thermals, you soar overhead. They can see you and they look up as you would if an eagle were to soar over you. You circle over them watching every little piece of their lives and their world.

While you are soaring overhead, you notice a field. Slowly rising from the field comes another bird. This one is the same size as you and it is creamy white. At a distance, it circles you. It sweeps in and away again, not threatening, just playing. It has flown past and is turning. You see that it has something in its beak. It is a piece of card. This time as it rushes past you it turns its head as though to ask you to take this piece of card. As it turns again you remain still and as it passes you, you reach out and take the card.

The bird sweeps around once more before descending back to the field and out of sight. The people are watching you and as you begin to soar again you sense that they wish you well. You circle low overhead, dip your wings and fly back over the ocean.

As you do so, the sky turns to a reddish glow and night falls. It is a warm night and soon you find yourself flying over the cliffs and towards the moonlit rolling hills behind them. You slow down, circle once more and land gently in a sheltered dip in a field corner.

You take the card and look at it. At first it appears to be plain, with nothing on it, but your eyes adjust to the moonlight and you begin to see tiny writing on it. The writing is so small, as if the people on the distant land had written it, thinking you too were very small which you must have seemed as you soared overhead. You hold the card close to your eyes and you read it.

You feel moved by the words. They have meaning to you. What does the writing say?

Slowly feel yourself stirring. Wiggle your toes and clench and relax your hands. Stretch your body. When you are ready, if your eyes were closed open them.

Spend a few minutes reflecting. There were many pieces of this script that were left open to you to visualize. How did you fill in the gaps? How do you interpret this?

Meditation

Meditation is another practice that has strong social norms associated with it. Most religions have a comparable practice, although it is probably the Buddhist faith that, in European eyes, is most commonly linked with this way of connecting with an altered state of consciousness.

In essence, meditation involves spending a period of time concentrating deeply on an aspect of yourself or a single thought to the point of actively excluding other thoughts. This is not easy and requires practice. The result is a shift from a confused mind struggling to manage many different things at once to one that is focused on a single aspect and can devote all of its energies to it.

To begin with most people meditate for 20 or 30 minutes. This may sound like a long time to sit and do nothing, but consider the amount of time you spend watching television! Most people think nothing of watching a half hour of a distressing news bulletin that does little to improve their well-being and usually leaves them frustrated or upset. So spending 20 minutes increasing your awareness and improving your mental and physical health is relatively little considering the return!

We are going to give simple instructions to begin two of the most widely known approaches. If you find this area interesting then you will find countless books in your local bookshop on the approach or you can browse the Internet and find many millions of Web pages devoted to it.

For any meditation, it is important that you find somewhere that you will feel comfortable in, are unlikely to be disturbed and will be safe. If necessary ask for your family's co-operation.

Zen meditation

In this meditation you concentrate on your breathing. This will give you something to focus on and help you to remain in a meditative state so it is perhaps a slightly easier one to begin with.

1. Sit upright comfortably – don't worry about adopting a cross-legged position for now.
2. Close your eyes and relax.
3. Breathe from your stomach with emphasis on the outward breath. Exhale slowly until you feel as though you have really emptied your lungs.
4. Inhale in a relaxed way, simply allowing your lungs to fill to their normal capacity.
5. Keep your mind perfectly clear. Don't let any thoughts intrude. Just breathe.
6. If you have difficulty clearing your mind, count your breaths up to 10 and then start again.
7. Do this for at least 20 minutes!

Zen philosophies are among the most difficult to encapsulate without distorting. The general aim of practising Zen is liberation. As one of their great philosophers, Lao-tzu said, 'Become unaffected; cherish sincerity; belittle the personal; reduce desires.' The subject of God is not addressed.

Yoga meditation

This meditation is easy to teach but difficult to maintain because there are no mental images on which to focus. So your mind will probably wander. Don't be put off – allow yourself time to learn and experience it.

1. Sit upright comfortably – don't worry about adopting a cross-legged position for now.
2. Close your eyes, take a few deep breaths, and relax.

3. Focus your attention on a spot in the middle of your forehead.
4. Keep your mind perfectly clear. Try not to let any thoughts
   intrude. Concentrate only on the middle of your forehead.
5. Try to do this for 20 minutes!

Lucky accidents and things that go wrong

Just as dreams can reflect our unconscious, so can a number of
other events. The well-known examples are Freudian slips. One
advertising campaign has recently focused on this to promote
Guinness with an actor playing an estate agent giving a guided
tour around a house and frequently making references through
slips to the beer! Another example though is the fortunate or lucky
accident.

For example, instead of going to somewhere you don't want to
go, you make a mistake and end up where you would rather be. I
remember as a young boy being asked by my grandmother to take
some flowers to one of her neighbours. I'm sure that I didn't deliberately take them to the wrong one, I simply ended up giving them
to the neighbour I liked rather than one I didn't!

Then there's the perpetual problem that almost certainly says
something about an unconscious wish. I had one customer that I
had to go and see, but for some reason, I tried three times to get
there – the first time I took the wrong junction at the motorway, the
second, I was so late leaving that I couldn't possibly get there, and
on the third, the motorway was closed due to an accident but I
hadn't heard the traffic report on the radio and ended up stuck in
traffic! Go on, be honest, you've done similar things.

A colleague of mine was travelling north from London to
Manchester. There was supposed to be a gathering of a team in
Birmingham in the evening, but his early morning commitments
meant he couldn't stop off. You can imagine our surprise when he
walked into our hotel lobby and said he was staying after all. It
turned out that he had had a flat tyre on the roundabout immediately outside and for some reason couldn't get it fixed until the
morning.

As Freud would have it, nothing in life is a coincidence. If you
think something is, then interpret it.

NOTES

1   Sperry, R W (1966) Brain bisection and mechanisms of consciousness, *in Brain and Conscious Experience*, ed J C Eccles, Springer Verlag, Berlin

2   Osborne, R (1993) *Freud for Beginners*, Writers and Readers, New York

3   Edwards, B (1993) *Drawing on the Right Side of the Brain*, HarperCollins, London

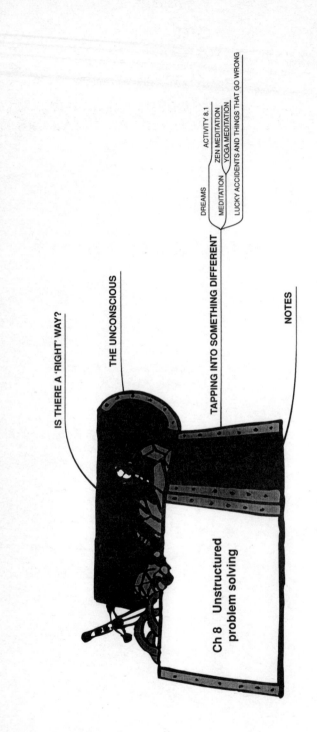

IS THERE A 'RIGHT' WAY?

THE UNCONSCIOUS

TAPPING INTO SOMETHING DIFFERENT

DREAMS

ACTIVITY 8.1

MEDITATION

ZEN MEDITATION

YOGA MEDITATION

LUCKY ACCIDENTS AND THINGS THAT GO WRONG

NOTES

Ch 8   Unstructured problem solving

Figure 8.1   *Overview of Chapter 8*

CHAPTER 9

Problem-solving models

WHY DO WE NEED PROBLEM-SOLVING MODELS?

It might surprise you that most managers are thought to be addressing between 50 and 70 problems at any one time.[1] There is also evidence, from brain biology, that most of us have difficulty juggling more than eight or nine significant topics at once – and at least one of those will be home life – you will begin to recognize that some of these problems are relatively insignificant.

In many professions, a structured approach is taught as a basic requirement for the work. Examples include the police force, medicine, law, engineering and the military. In recent years, there has been a growing interest in the use of systematic approaches to day-to-day work. This has culminated in the international standard, ISO9000, which is really a structure for structures!

Whole professions have emerged based on structured approaches. A few decades ago work study offered a means of improving productivity based on systematic approaches to work. More recently we saw the growth of systems analysis as information technology began to take off.

There are many reasons for the prevalence of structured approaches:

1. They remove ambiguity.
2. They reduce individual bias.
3. They reduce the need for experience and judgement.
4. They ensure rigour.
5. They can improve communication.
6. They facilitate handover.

7. They make third party assessment easier.
8. They give an impression that work is 'on track'.
9. They avoid extraneous activity.

Clearly, such models do have a role to play, but they should be used with an open mind. There are probably just as many ways of working in an unstructured way as there are in a structured one. Simply because we have 'always done it that way' doesn't mean that we should continue to do so today.

THE PHASES OF A PROBLEM-SOLVING MODEL

Many different problem-solving models are taught on management development courses. They are all essentially the same, despite the claims of their proponents. Any problem-solving model begins with a definition of the problem, then uses divergent thinking techniques to develop possible solutions before using convergent techniques to identify the best solution, implement it and test its effectiveness.

The divergent phase expands the problem. The team members define what they are trying to tackle and determine some boundaries. They decide how to measure their success and find out as much as they can about the problem as they have defined it. Most of the creative effort is concentrated on this phase. The person who is acting in the role of Co-ordinator (as defined by Belbin, 1981) will be calling particularly on people with Plant and Shaper tendencies. The techniques used by the team will try to make use of their right-brain faculties.

It is widely reported that Japanese managers spend more time in this phase than those in the West do. Whether this is really the case is difficult to establish, but there are a number of techniques which originated in Japan that do encourage their users to spend more time expanding the problem. One example is QFD, a technique developed at the Kobe Shipyards as a tool for improving the customer focus of products and services. For a thorough explanation of this technique and its application, see Wilson (1993).[2]

The convergent phase common to problem-solving models allows the team to develop its solution. The immediate reaction of students on MBA courses is often surprise that convergent thinking should be applied to develop a solution. They have been brought up to expect some flash of inspiration, a radical side-step, or lateral thinking.

As Conan Doyle illustrated in his Sherlock Holmes stories, most problems are resolved when all the facts are known about them. It is necessary to possess keen powers of observation and to analyse the facts thoroughly – then solutions become very obvious. In many cases teams find that simply describing their problem properly gives them the solution.

Thus the convergent phase of a problem-solving model is more concerned with developing the practical aspects of implementing a solution that became obvious much earlier. In doing this the left-brain powers of reasoning and structured thought will be called on. The key is to develop solutions that can be put into practice and to find the necessary resources. The team roles called for here will be Monitor/Evaluators, Team Workers, Company Workers, and Completer/Finishers.

Again, this is often regarded as a stage of low effort in Japanese businesses, whereas in the West not to invest effort here is often seen as a fault – 'fiddling while Rome burns'! Figure 9.1 illustrates these different approaches to problem-solving.

I'm happy with the model I already have!

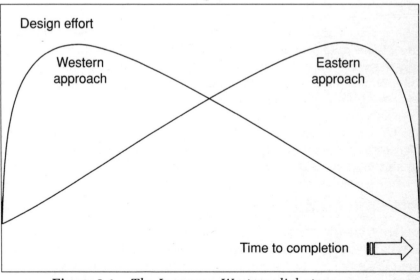

Figure 9.1   *The Japanese–Western dichotomy over problem solving*

Problem-solving models are often taught on courses early in a person's career, but are not adequately understood and therefore are not applied. To help you recall your own training and see the similarities between approaches, Table 9.1 is a comparison of the most common approaches. The GOAL model has been taught on courses influenced by the work of W Edwards Deming; Coverdale run training programmes on 'systematic working'; and Francis's approach is taught at Henley – The Management College.

A frequent difficulty encountered with problem-solving models, and the reason that most solutions created using them don't work, is that people omit stages from the process. They may jump from identifying the problem to deciding on a solution without exploring alternatives, or they may not include a final evaluation process.

Activity 9.1

If you have come across other models, such as those of Kepner-Tregoe,[3] annotate Table 9.1 accordingly. Try analysing a successful project and ask yourself what happened at each stage.

PRIDE

The approach that I prefer is the PRIDE model. This is a variation of the PRICE model developed by Ken Blanchard.[4] It does not have any magical powers. As you will see from Table 9.1, it has nothing that other models do not also have. However, being a mnemonic it is easier to remember without notes and is therefore more likely to be used.

The basic stages of the PRIDE model are described below. Subsequent chapters will consider the different tools and techniques used in its application.

PINPOINT the problem

Before trying to tackle any problem it is important to move away from its symptoms – which are usually seen as the problem by most people anyway – to the underlying issue. Even with a very clear brief, most problem-solving teams will have a range of ideas on the 'real' issue.

Table 9.1 *Comparison of some common problem-solving models*

PRIDE	Blanchard	Francix	Coverdale	GOAL
Pinpoint	Pinpoint	Tuning in	Purposes	To decide which problem will be addressed first (or next)
		Objective setting	End results	To arrive at a statement that describes the problem in terms of what it is specifically, where it occurs, when it happens, and its extent
		Success measures	Success criteria or results	
Record	Record	Information collection	Information	To develop a complete picture of all the possible causes of the problem
Inform yourselves and others	Involve	Decision–making		To agree on the basic cause(s) of the problem
Decide		Planning	Plan	To develop an effective and implementable solution and action plan
Effect	Coach	Action	Action, Do it!	To implement the solution and establish required monitoring procedures and charts
Evaluate	Evaluate	Review to improve		

For example, early in my career I was asked to help reduce absenteeism in one group of employees in a particular company. Even phrased more positively – improving their attendance – this was not the real issue. The real problem lay in a number of policies that the employees perceived as undermining their status within the company.

RECORDING information

After defining the problem clearly, you then gather information to help you understand it better. Some authors will tell you to stick to 'facts' and not get sidetracked by opinions. To us an opinion is one person's version of the facts and has just as much value in this data collection process. Exactly which 'facts' are needed has to be decided by the team. Several approaches to this are described in Chapter 11.

INFORMING ourselves and others

Armed with a list of requirements, the group members set about gathering information. The object is to expand their understanding of the problem. In doing so they will be involved in contact with other people. This is often an opportunity to prepare the ground for testing solutions and to improve people's overall understanding of the change process. For some reason, groups sometimes develop elaborate plots to avoid telling others what they are doing and why. This does not work and should be avoided.

Data selection, data collection and analysis are all important steps in the development of an effective solution. They are also potentially the most expensive and easiest to get wrong. The team may need to prepare itself carefully by looking at techniques of phrasing questions, designing questionnaires and planning surveys.[5]

DECIDING on and DESIGNING a solution

The last phase of divergent thinking that the team is involved in is devising solutions to the problem that will respond to the facts that they have gathered. This process is often not as difficult as it sounds – solutions tend to suggest themselves out of the data collected.

EFFECT the solution

Although the team may not be expected to put its recommendations into practice, it does need to devise appropriate ways of introducing them. Sometimes this can call for considerable effort and
should not be underestimated. After all, many businesses recognize
the need to reduce their bureaucracy; the real problem is how to
achieve a reduction.

EVALUATE the results

No solution is complete without a method of assessing its impact.
The second by-product of the data collection process is the identi-
fication of a small number of key indicators that will show whether
or not the team's recommendations have been successful.

DO WE NEED TO REPORT TO SOMEONE ELSE?

Once they have completed their study, developed their preferred
solution(s), and devised plans for implementation and monitoring,
then some teams will need to report back to their sponsors.

Usually the team's report will consist of three elements:

■ a physical presentation;
■ copies of the material used in the presentation;
■ a supporting document, containing the important data and
evidence.

The presentation is crucial. A poorly made presentation will be
uninspiring, may reinforce doubts that the approach will not work,
and can set the organization back a long way. Most teams use
straightforward presentation materials, but there are exceptions.
Among the alternatives are videos, scale models, site tours and
visits to other organizations (Disney seems very popular!).

Some time needs to be set aside to prepare the report, and the
process should begin virtually as soon as the team has agreed its
primary tasks. It is important to provide the sponsors with copies
of the presentation material. We are often asked whether this
should be done before or after the presentation. Usually teams
prefer to give the materials out at the beginning of the presentation

so that the audience can make notes. Unfortunately there are a few people who will turn to the back of a pack, read the conclusions and then ask obscure questions about information that is going to be given later in the presentation. If you suspect that you have one of these people in your audience, prepare beforehand and be ready to put them in their place politely!

Questions are probably best handled at the end of the presentation, when they can be directed to other members of the team. Finally the report should be given to the sponsors. It is usually best to take a copy for everyone rather than circulating a single copy.

NOTES

1   Mintzberg, H (1973) *The Nature of Managerial Work*, Prentice-Hall, Englewood Cliffs

2   Wilson, G B (1993) *On Route to Perfection*, IFS Publications, Bedford

3   Kepner, C H and Tregoe, B B (1986) *The Rational Manager*, Kepner-Tregoe, Boston

4   Blanchard, K and Lorber, R (1984) *Putting the One Minute Manager to Work*, Willow Books, New York

5   Oppenheim, A N (1966) *Questionnaire Design and Attitude Measurement*, Heinemann, London

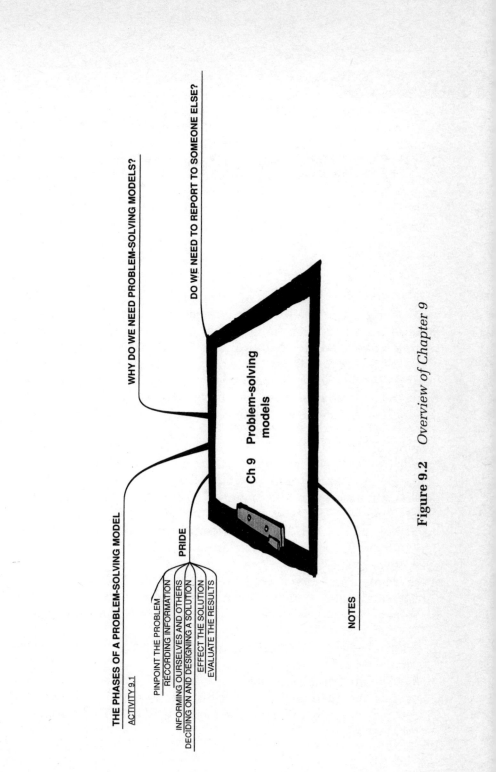

Figure 9.2 *Overview of Chapter 9*

CHAPTER 10

Pinpointing the problem

This chapter discusses tools and techniques for pinpointing the exact problem that needs to be addressed. The remaining chapters describe a variety of techniques that may be of use in problem solving. They are divided according to the five stages of the PRIDE problem-solving model but this does not mean that they will only be useful at one stage. Some occasions when a particular tool is likely to be of use have been identified, but you will probably find it helpful to read about all the tools so that you can spot opportunities to do so when they come up.

Some of the techniques are well known, others are not too familiar. Some are very simple, others are too complex to give a definitive description here, in which case details are given where you can find out more information. You may find that some techniques appear so complex that they are beyond the grasp of any problem-solving team. If you are tempted to call in an outsider, bear in mind the guidelines given in Chapter 4.

Practical examples have been included where appropriate, but these chapters are intended to be like a toolbox and not a manufacturer's maintenance manual. If you feel that more detail is required before you can use a particular tool, then do one of the following:

1. Try using the tool on a simple example – some activities have been included to help you with this.
2. Review what you were planning to do with it to see if you have over-complicated matters – simplify and try again.
3. Ask for help – there's always someone who has faced a similar problem.

One other point about these tools and techniques. For simplicity the terminology of a process has been adopted. This is not meant to imply that they are only applicable in production environments. Quite the contrary – every technique works just as well in a service organization.

CONSEQUENCE LISTING

It is often very difficult to put into words what a problem involves. This can be because the issue is very obscure, complex, or outside your experience. You might be sure about only what the situation is now and how you would prefer it to be. This is what consequence listing is about. Incidentally, consequence listing is also a good tool to work through with individuals as it can help them focus on how they would like their lives to be different.

In a team-based setting, as a team, draw up a list of the present characteristics of your situation. Brainstorming is a good way of doing this as it breaks the ice and starts communication between people. Writing the list with a red pen lends it impact. Leave a reasonable space between items. Depending on the team and its levels of energy and participation, you may want to use a whole flip-chart sheet for this or divide it into two columns.

Now work down the list again using a green pen and writing alongside each item how the team members expect the situation to change. You can expect there to be confusion and you might feel tempted to pass judgement as to whether items are really character-istics of the 'new world', solutions, or an individual members 'wish list' – avoid stepping in!

Once the list is fairly comprehensive, the team can discuss how to reduce it to what it considers are core statements of the problem. Some people say that this process works well for them in reverse – listing the consequences before the conditions. This seems logical, but it can lead to a sense of gloom and despondency that it may be better to avoid, especially at the first meeting of the team.

SYSTEMS ANALYSIS

In many organizations where left-brain thinking predominates, a highly structured approach is called for by the sponsors of the problem-solving activity. Such organizations seem to measure the value of a technique not by its results but by its complexity and the quality of printing of the instructions! A lot could be gained by challenging this. However, there are techniques that pander to the need.

In this kind of environment an excellent approach for pinpointing problems is systems analysis. There are several forms of systems analysis. The professional's tools that include SSADM are undoubtedly effective but I prefer simple methods that a team can carry out, benefiting from speed and ownership at the cost of detail.

Handling information

One of the commonest problems facing people at work today is an excess of information – what to do with it, how to store it, and so on. Whether it is considered a problem or not, most people are exposed to a wealth of information in their daily lives. Some of it is useful, some useless and much of it is in between.

There is some evidence that badly organized information is a serious source of stress for many managers. Certainly most management trainers report that the principal cause of poor time management is a lack of organization of information.

At the individual level the consequences of this disorganization are often poor delegation, failure to meet deadlines, inaccurate reports, and poor quality. For this reason, many problem-solving teams find themselves investigating issues that reflect 'information overload'. Teams are not exempt from this either – many have floundered because of 'analysis paralysis'.

How to handle a large amount of information is a question that has been puzzling people for years. Of course, there are already some solutions: newspapers, books and journals all synthesize information and present it in a summary form. As a consultant I like to review the recent press comments about a company before I meet its directors. Ten years ago, doing this involved a lot of personal effort and the expense of a cuttings service. Five or six years ago, it was easy to go 'online' search for electronic copies of the same journals and papers and download the actual text of the articles. Today, these electronic copies have mostly disappeared. The publishers have had to embrace the Internet and now offer two versions – one for paper and the other for Internet publishing. Most national newspapers today have two editions and it is increasingly common to see people commuting to work reading their 'paper' off a laptop computer.

Day-to-day information in the office has also gone through an IT revolution. A few years ago you could measure the volume of paper that landed on many managers' desks in kilograms. Today much of this will be electronic, through office automation systems, company accounting systems, personal information managers, lead tracking systems, and so on. The latest generation is Internet linked and carries graphics, sound and video. So how can a problem-solving team tackle problems that are perhaps caused by such information overload, certainly are masked by so much data, and require extensive research?

Taking notes

There are distinct benefits to be gained from making summary notes rather than relying on the original data. Evidence gathered by Michael Howe[1] at the University of Exeter in the 1970s showed that the fact that a person makes notes improves his or her recall by a factor of six.

This is one reason why the old trick practised by sales represen-tatives works so well. Sales reps have long been taught to keep a dictation machine in their car. As soon as they can after leaving the customer they dictate into the recorder their comments about the visit. Everything is recorded, even trivia such as where the contact has been on holiday, or the ages and progress of their children. Then before visiting the client next time, they play back the last few minutes of the tape. Their recall is already much greater than it would have been because they recorded the information – the play-back simply acts as a trigger. Keeping notes means that information can be encoded, organized and reorganized. It also enables someone to focus on the important points rather than the extra-neous material.

Howe's work went on to look at the effectiveness of different note-taking styles. In examinations students are expected to communicate in prose, with properly constructed sentences, main-taining a reasonable level of conformity to grammatical rules. Funnily enough, the same applies in the non-academic world! Some managers even believe that it is their job to correct the written language of their employees.

People's ability to recall information is related to certain aspects of the written form. If you listen to small children speaking, they use few words and incomplete sentences. They can usually be understood because of the context in which they are at the time. They use mainly nouns and verbs and rarely conjunctions, adjectives or pronouns. It can be shown that languages evolve by increasing complexity through the use of 'padding' words. Thus modern languages are worse than Latin, and they are all worse than Sanskrit. It is therefore not surprising that an individual's ability to recall information is related to the proportion of key words in the text being studied.

Traditional text is linear, running across and down the page and from front to back cover. This is acceptable if you are a structured linear thinker ('left-brain dominant'), but not so convenient if you are right-brain dominant and prefer to see the larger picture at once.

Text has quite a few other problems associated with it. Roughly 90–95 per cent of the words will have no bearing on the meaning; they are 'pad words'. This means that the reader's attention tends to wander unless the text is really exciting. Recall will be poorer. If the text is in the form of notes, intermediate points will tend to be missed. Time is also wasted in taking the notes, rereading them and filing them. Two other problems exist with linear notes, especially when they are printed. First, any drawings or charts tend to get separated from the text that refers to them. This means that the reader has to jump backwards and forwards, reinforcing all the problems that have already been described above. The second is not so much a problem as a lost opportunity. When you are explaining something to someone else it is useful to produce joint notes – this makes sure that both of you are using the same information. With linear notes this can be time-consuming, expensive and inconvenient, and if the other person normally speaks another language then it is very difficult to make sure that you have both understood the same things.

Teams solving problems often find themselves having to make notes and share information with one another. Imagine how much more creative they could be if they had 20 times more time to work on the problem while at the same time possessing identical notes that they had all contributed to together!

Mind mapping

In 1974 the psychologist Tony Buzan published a book[2] that was to make popular a simple alternative to linear notes. He built on a technique that people had experimented with for centuries but which had never really become popular. Today the approach has many advocates and can be a powerful tool for anyone wanting to distil large quantities of information. As his approach was designed to appeal to right-brain as well as left-brain dominant people and was generally more sympathetic to the way the mind works, Buzan called it 'mind mapping'.

Anecdotal and quantitative evidence is slowly accumulating that the method produces dramatic improvements in people's ability to make use of quite complex information. There are a small number of computer systems available for creating mind maps, although the technology will continue to develop. This book was created entirely within one of these programs and the mind maps at the end of each chapter were prepared as part of this process using the same package.

Many words take their meaning from the context in which they are used and who is using them. Therefore any note-taking technique has to put words in the right context. This is the main role of the 'pad words' in traditional linear notes. Mind mapping not only does this but draws on the right brain's ability to build associations between objects and concepts.

Several studies of 20th-century innovation, commercial and otherwise, have shown that most modern inventions or solutions to problems arise through hitherto unthought of connections between concepts.[3] Thus, for example, the popular application of incandescent light only arose owing to its transformation from a safety device onboard wooden ships to floodlighting for baseball! Alistair Cook's *Letter from America* radio programme, for instance, has used the same formula for half a century, addressing two seemingly distinct themes and linking them together.

Producing mind maps

The mind mapping approach begins with a blank sheet of paper. In the centre is written the central theme – a title. To make this visually appealing it may have a simple sketch added to it. In the notes for this chapter the central image is a flying saucer casting a beam of light onto the title. Arranged around the central title are key themes. You may not identify all of these at first, but the notes can be built up as you add to your knowledge. Each theme can have branches and sub-branches *ad infinitum*, or at least until you run out of space.

The words making up the themes are deliberately kept short, rarely more than one or two, and they are usually written only in UPPER CASE. This is to ensure legibility and also provides a slightly longer time for the information and its associations to register in the mind of the person drawing the chart.

You can enhance the chart through simple graphics, line drawings or by using colour. Some people prefer to use colours to associate items across the mind map, while others simply use them to separate the themes.

The benefits of mind mapping stem from the patterns that it produces and the way that the mind uses them. First, it allows connections between themes to be made visual, which they would never be in written text. Then it allows clusters of information about common issues to be kept together, not scattered across several pages. The pattern of the images on a piece of paper appeals to visual memory, which means that you recall not only the subject matter but also what it looks like. Stepping in for a sick colleague, I recently had to give a particular talk to a group of people for the first time in three years. The only notes were in the form of a mind map and there was no time to study it. But as soon as the first couple of themes had been examined the rest came flooding back – right down to a spelling mistake on one of the branches!

The production of mind maps is simple and there is no need to stick to rigid rules. The whole idea is to be creative. With the 'pad words' taken out, a surprising amount of information can be included on one sheet of paper. Typically I expect to summarize the content of 200 pages of conceptual information on one side of A4 – although I may 'cheat' slightly by starting with an A3 sheet and reducing it on a photocopier. For a fun introduction to mind maps look for the video by Lana Israel.[4] If you prefer to use a computer to do your mind mapping you might investigate the *Mind Manager* software, which was used to create this book.[5]

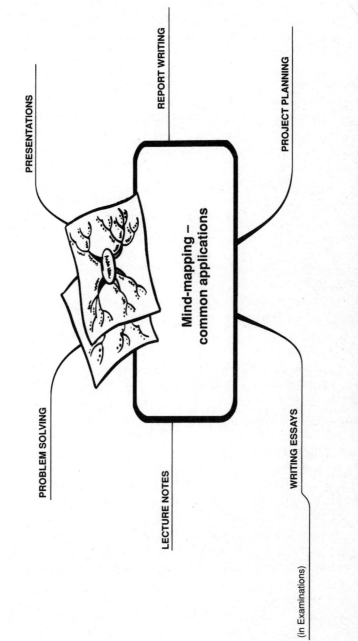

Figure 10.1 *Common applications of mind mapping*

Applications

The applications of mind maps are widespread – any situation in which you want to keep notes is a suitable target. Some of the more popular are shown in Figure 10.1.

Project planning

You have been called into the managing director's office and given a briefing for a new project. As the managing director talks, you jot down the start of a mind map. As you are only noting key words you can give more attention to the briefing.

With the basic mind map started, you go and get a beaker of coffee from the machine, return to your office and ruminate on the features of the project. If you follow a standard project management system you may use the components of this as your main themes. Alternatively you might use a problems-solving model like those described in Chapter 9.

As you build up the mind map you realize that the sheet of A4 is going to be too limiting, so you nip along the corridor and copy it at the centre of a sheet of A3. Over the morning you build on it. You ring up a friend and ask if they would mind talking it through with you over lunch in the canteen – you can do this because although linear notes would be too cumbersome by now, the A3 page will easily spread across the table. Over lunch you add to the mind map, resisting the temptation to creep over onto the table-cloth!

Back in the office, you attach the A3 sheet to your whiteboard or flip-chart easel and continue to develop it. All this time you are not only adding ideas to the various themes but also reviewing the other information.

By the time that you are ready to start taking action you have a clear picture of all the ramifications of the project, who will be affected by it, when to involve different people, and so on. Now you can transcribe relevant items to other formal documents such as flowcharts, resource allocation sheets or project approval forms, safe in the knowledge that little or nothing can be missed.

Group note taking

Still working on the project, you call together the team of people who will be responsible for it. You give them a briefing – more on this in a moment – and suggest that you should all pool your thoughts on what needs to be done. Using a flip-chart sheet (A1) on the table in front of you, you write the project name in the middle. As each person contributes a comment or idea, he or she summarizes it in a couple of words and records it on the flip-chart paper in the form of a mind map.

By the end of the meeting you will have a thorough set of notes that everyone has contributed to and reviewed several times. Rolling it up, you take it back to the office with you. On the way home that evening you pop into the local plan copy shop – if you don't know one call any architect and ask them where they get their plans copied. The shop will reduce the A1 sheet down to A3 or even A4 for less than a couple of pounds and you can then copy this and circulate it when you get to the office the following day. Incidentally, most plan copy shops offer a door-to-door service at no extra cost – if you make extensive use of this technique they are worth getting to know!

There are a number of situations that can arise where it isn't possible for all the team to get together in one place. Nowadays a growing number of companies use tele-conferencing to communicate between locations. Some tele-conferencing suites have sophisticated white-boards that can be linked up in different offices so that anything drawn on one appears on the other and vice versa. If your company doesn't have one, you might consider using the facility at one of the communications shops, or serviced offices that are appearing in many city centres. Another technological solution is to use one of the PC-based mind mapping tools described earlier. At least one of these has an Internet tool to allow people to simultaneously add ideas to the same map.

Later in the project you can use mind mapping as a straightforward substitute for fishbone diagrams (see Chapter 11). Drawing connections and structuring information in this way are much more flexible. It is also an easier technique to use than verbal brainstorming in any small group.

Structured brainstorming

As a problem-solving tool, mind mapping is a good way of representing the ideas of a group. Sometimes the size of a group makes it difficult to write legibly and capture all the ideas that are flowing. In my experience the best way of using mind mapping to do this is to equip everyone with a pad of small Post-it Notes and a dark fibre-tipped pen. Lay the flip-chart paper horizontally on the table in front of the group (perhaps someone one day will produce land-scape format flip-chart easels!).

Write a simple theme statement in the centre of the chart in reasonably small letters – it doesn't have to be read from the far side of the room. Each person can then add their ideas to the chart, writing on the Post-it Notes so that they can be relocated if neces-sary. There is no need for any rigorous rules like one person at a time, or asking, 'Where would you like this to go?' every time someone makes a contribution. Let the group find a style that it is comfortable with. Once the stream of new ideas has dried up, discuss how to rearrange the notes. Eventually add lines to the mind map to complete the picture.

If you intend photocopying the flip-chart sheet so that everyone can have a copy, draw lines halfway across in both directions dividing the sheet into A4 areas. Agree that Post-its can be placed adjacent to the lines but not across them. This will make it much easier to fold the sheet for copying on a standard office photo-copier.

Communication
At various stages in a problem-solving team's deliberations they will have to communicate with other people. Generally, the more they communicate the better. Unfortunately, the time that it takes to prepare a presentation or write an interim report can begin to detract from the core work of the group. Mind mapping provides an excellent way of reducing the time and yet being more effective in the process.

Presentations
Most people have to make a presentation from time to time. Everyone knows that you should not write a script and read it out, but many people find the idea of presenting to a group daunting.

Draw up a mind map of the subjects you are going to cover and copy it in black and white. Then put rings of colour around a few key concepts that will form the core of your presentation. Now decide on the order in which you will present them and label the clusters accordingly.

Make up a less detailed mind map using the same shape and colours, but with fewer key words. Now practise the presentation using this second mind map. If you find yourself stumbling, add a few more words to the relevant area and repeat that part of the presentation. Once you are confident that you have sufficient words to base your talk on and have run through the talk a couple of times yourself, you can transcribe the words that you have put on your mind map onto charts for either an overhead or a 35mm projector.

Not only have you practised the presentation, but you have tailored the material to your style of speaking and not the other way round. This is one of the commonest problems that people have when making presentations. They lose their place in their notes, forget why they have included a particular chart, or have not had sufficient practice. You have covered all three in a fraction of the time.

Report writing
Hopefully by now you will have begun to question whether a report should be written at all. After all, why not present people with a mind map instead? Assuming that there are valid reasons why a textual document has to be prepared, then the approach to writing a report is similar to that for giving presentations. Copy the main mind map and then colour clusters that form distinct topics.

Label the sequence of these clusters and begin writing. It really is as easy as that. The problem that you have overcome is that you no longer need to refer back to the original volumes and sift the information. If you like dictating then it is even easier; all you have to do is 'read' from the mind map.

Flow charts

Most people have seen flow charts at some time. If the group is tackling a problem with some kind of linear structure to it, such as one concerning production, logistics, administration, or service delivery, then flow charting can be useful. Figure 10.2 is a typical example.

During the discussion the team builds up a picture of the major activities involved. Some symbols need to be agreed: conventionally, start and end points are drawn as long oblongs with rounded ends; activities as rectangles; stores as ovals; decisions as diamonds. Each step is linked to another by lines with arrows to show the direction. As before, a flip-chart on the table and Post-it Notes are a handy way of recording information as they give people a chance to reposition items.

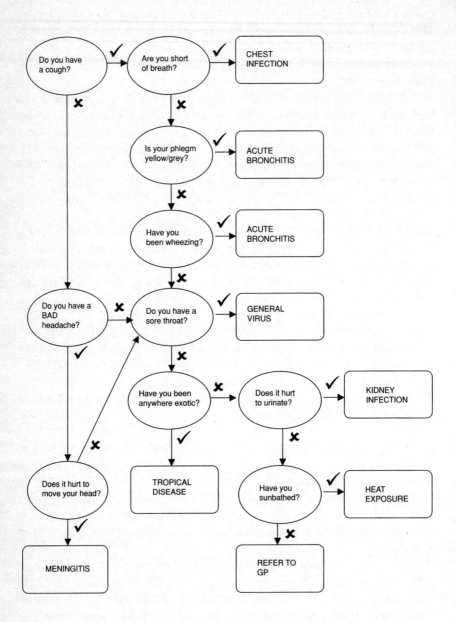

Figure 10.2   *A typical flow chart*

Two problems need to be avoided with this approach. First, you may be tempted to use an internal expert on the flow chart process to draw up the diagram. This may be educational but it does not help the group learn to work together. It can also put that person in a position of power.

Second, do not allow the group to assume that it has produced the definitive flow chart. Some organizations are far more complex than anyone initially thinks, others are just very bad at allowing people to know what is involved. One group of senior managers in a small company with only 100 employees drew a flow chart of the company's activities. When they saw the chart that had been prepared by the supervisors by 'walking the job' they could barely believe their own ignorance!

Armed with a flow chart, the group can begin to discuss where problems might be occurring that could cause the symptoms it is trying to tackle. This often provides the basis for some simple data collection to verify the assumptions and can quickly lead a team into its core work.

Wherever the physical movement of stock or information occurs, a particular variation of the flow chart can be invaluable. The team uses a simple plan of the premises, or the country if that is the scale that is necessary (for sales problems perhaps), and transfers the flow chart to the map or builds it up on the map from scratch.

This approach has tremendous potential. Barriers to effective working leap out of the paper. In a double glazing factory, for example, units were being transported 8 kilometres in a production process that only needed 30 metres. In a textile yarn manufacturers a production process that originally took six weeks was reduced to two days. In a German sales office, individually typed letters 'walked' 2 kilometres for signature and 2 kilometres back!

ONGOING RECORDS

Often organizations have abundant supplies of information. Most of it will be irrelevant to the team, but it can sometimes be of use if it is assembled by the leader before the group begins to pinpoint the problem. The leader should not spend long analysing the information; if the group carries out the analysis everyone can share in the discovery.

Data of this kind can be useful in establishing a background level for a problem against which the team can measure its own success. The team may want to develop some simple run charts or more formal control charts, or they may decide on areas of particular interest and introduce a short-term log so that problems become more visible.

Logbooks

The logbook is a simple idea and many companies use them already. The book is a record of everything that happens in a particular area documented chronologically. With some discipline, most people find that maintaining a logbook is relatively easy.

Some people consider logbooks an invaluable briefing tool for people on different shifts, others for dealing with suppliers. Team members can use the data to provide quantitative information about the frequency of problems and the duration of certain events.

Run charts

When you want to display the simplest form of trend between observation points, a run chart allows you to see whether or not the long-term average is changing. Points are plotted on the graph in the order that they occur. All sorts of information can be displayed in this manner: machine downtime, delivery times, yield, scrap, productivity, and so on.

The disadvantage of run charts is that they can make people see every variation as significant. Their real benefit is in highlighting potential sources of problems and dismissing those that are red herrings. Some people seem to think that run charts are not as accurate as control charts, but this is not the case.

If you have calculated an average for the process and then record successive points, a run of nine points on one side of the average indicates a significant deviation and can be used to alert the team quickly. Alternatively, similar significance can be attached to a trend of six points in one direction, either upwards or downwards, regardless of where the average is.

Control charts

A control chart is simply a run chart with statistically determined upper and lower lines drawn on either side of the process average. These limits are calculated by running the process without disturbing it, taking samples regularly, and then carrying out some simple calculations. The subsequent sample averages are then plotted on the chart to determine whether any of them lie outside the limits or fall foul of the runs rules. If this is the case, the process is said to be out of control. This is a slight misnomer as there are many circumstances under which the averages might begin to change legitimately.

The variation within the limits is said to come from 'common causes'. In the past this was said to be natural variation and could not be reduced. The variation outside the limits either comes from 'irregular causes', one-off problems that the team should address, or from 'special causes'. This last type of variation might include external influences such as deliberate changes in supplier, seasonal patterns or working patterns. Nowadays all sources of variation are seen as suitable for improvement. What used to be considered as natural variation is now open to investigation.

The form shown in Figure 10.3 can be used to produce a control chart of the kind described. For more information on producing statistical charts, in the modern way, refer to Wilson (1993).[6]

CHECK SHEETS

Most groups collect information about the problem before they really understand what the problem amounts to. For this reason one of the tools that they often use even at an early stage is the check sheet. By working as a team they can help move from opinions about the problem to facts.

Producing a check sheet is straightforward:

1. Agree exactly what will be observed.
2. Decide on the time to spend and the period to cover.
3. Design a form to record the information:
4. Ensure that everyone has the same form.
5. Ensure that all forms have a title.
6. Ensure that all forms show the date, time, place and person.
7. Make sure there is enough space in each column.
8. Ensure that all columns are properly labelled.

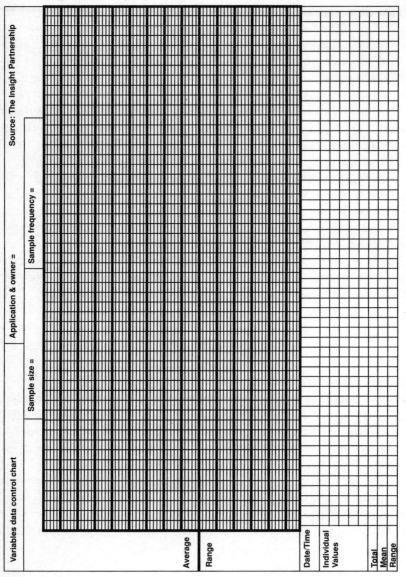

Figure 10.3 *A control chart*

9. Collect the data, ensuring that data samples are taken as randomly as possible.
10. Make sure that data collection is carried out efficiently.
11. Make sure that you are sampling from only one group (population); if not you need to subdivide first.
12. If the sampling is complex use a formal experiment.

There are probably hundreds of different types of check sheet. The four most common are:

1. Tally sheets.
2. Cumulative amounts.
3. Time and type.
4. Maps and diagrams.

Tally sheets

These consist of simple boxes in which a mark is made each time something in a particular category occurs. Most people draw four vertical lines and one diagonal for the fifth item, which makes it easy to calculate the final figures.

Cumulative amounts

Some problems involve an accumulation of data over consistent periods. In this case the columns represent each subsequent period (for example, 15-minute intervals) and the rows represent observations of different phenomena (for example, cars, lorries, bicycles, etc). This allows the data to be reanalysed without having to start from scratch each time.

Time and type

Often events cannot be predicted in terms of when they will happen, how often or even what they will be, such as customer complaints, accidents and machine breakdowns. For this sort of problem the team will use an open-ended form with columns to ensure that meaningful information is recorded, but without fixed rows.

Maps and diagrams

If a group has completed a flow chart or map because they are dealing with a logistical or similar problem, a simple enhancement can be very useful. Taking a skeleton of their map that people can understand, the team records the location of the problems. Usually tallies are marked as described above. This quickly highlights potential bottlenecks or unplanned storage areas.

SIGNIFICANCE ANALYSIS

The final tool in this section is another way of structuring discussions, rather like consequence listing. Significance analysis is concerned with deciding whether the team really ought to tackle the problem that it has identified.

Four columns are created, either on two sheets of paper or on four separate sheets arranged alongside one another. In the first column, team members put reasons that the problem is worth addressing. Next to this they estimate the relative importance of these reasons. They can do this by giving each a rating (1 to 5 or A, B, C) or they can rank them in a particular order, although this tends to be time-consuming and does not add much value.

In the third column, as a separate list, the team tries to say who ought to be involved in solving the problem. The idea of this is to identify problems that ought to be tackled by the only people who will benefit when they are not in the team. Common examples are problems that need senior managers to provide solutions, from which the only obvious beneficiaries will be the senior management team.

The final column is a list of the constraints that members of the team can envisage hampering them in their work. If many of these are outside their control and they are felt to outweigh the chances of achieving a satisfactory result, then now is the time to say *stop*!

The last stage in significance analysis is for the members of the team to consider the information and agree whether they *want* to tackle the problem. If not, then it is better for them to admit this and for a different team to take over than for the first team to proceed half-heartedly.

NOTES

1 Howe, M J A (1978) Using students' notes to examine the role of the individual learner in acquiring meaningful subject matter, *Journal of Educational Research*, **64**, pp 61–63

2   Buzan, T (1974) *Use your Head*, BBC, London

3   Jewkes, J, Sawyers, D and Stillerman, R (1982) *The Sources of Invention*, Pitman, London

4   Israel, L (1992) *Get Ahead*, Island World Communications, London. This is a video pack available from any good stationer. An excellent product, it makes mind maps accessible to everyone from itinerant youngsters to the crustiest of company chairmen!

5   *The Mind Manager* is a software tool for producing mind maps. This is the software used to write this book and allows remote conferencing via the Internet. The publisher's Web address is www.mindman.com

6   Wilson, G B (1993) *On Route to Perfection*, IFS, Bedford

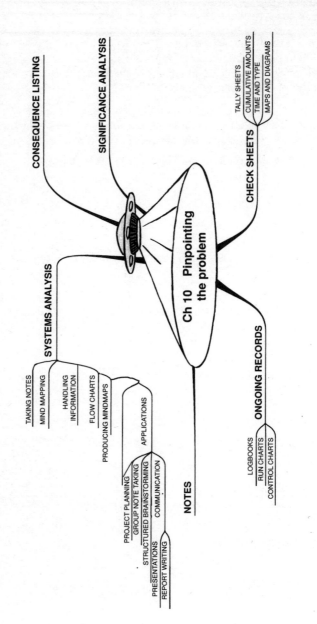

Figure 10.4 *Overview of Chapter 10*

CHAPTER 11

Recording data

Provided with a clear picture of the problem that they are tackling and the outcomes that they expect to achieve, the members of the team can begin to identify information that they need to collect. This information is put to use in a number of ways, the most obvious of which are:

- to confirm that the problem exists;
- to quantify potential problems and causes;
- to provide the basis of measured improvement;
- to establish potential solutions;
- to test the effectiveness of pilot solutions;
- to present a case for further action;
- to present a case for investment.

The data collected fall broadly into two types: numerical and textual. This does not mean that other types are excluded; such things as physical specimens, video and still photography, computer-generated images, and so on are all used regularly by teams. In this chapter we give details of a combination of these approaches. Do look at other chapters too for approaches that may be of use in your work.

CAUSE AND EFFECT DIAGRAMS

One of the techniques most widely associated with problem solving in Total Quality initiatives is the cause and effect diagram, also known as the Ishikawa diagram after its inventor, or the fishbone because of its shape. This is one of a family of techniques for developing structure in collections of mainly textual information. Cause and effect diagrams are a useful way of finding the cause of a problem.

The diagram consists of a pattern of arrows, each leading to another showing how each cause has an effect. There are several different forms of fishbone diagram and only the most common one will be described here, but they all work in a similar fashion.

First, decide on the main groups of causes. These form the 'bones' of the diagram (see Figure 11.1). It is usual to start with four main bones. You can name these yourself or you can use an existing pattern, such as:

- 4Ms: Manpower, Machines, Methods and Materials;
- 4Ps: Policies, Procedures, People and Plant;
- POEM: Plant, Operators, Equipment and Methods.

Figure 11.1

Choose whichever is the most appropriate for you. The procedure is then as follows:

1. Agree on one statement which describes the problem, specifically where, when or to what extent it occurs. This is the *effect* statement and is written in the fish's head.
2. Generate a list of possible causes by brainstorming.
3. Think over the ideas for a while (often as long as a week).
4. Agree on about four major causes (4Ms, 4Ps, POEM, etc).
5. Record the items from the brainstorming session on the fishbone chart under the major causes. Do not simply list them, try to create branching networks for each theme.
6. Build on the causes by adding sub-branches and asking yourself 'Why?' and 'How?'.
7. In the completed diagram look for common themes across branches.
8. Agree on the additional data that must be collected to establish the relative frequency or importance of causes *before* developing solutions.

Once the diagram is completed, the group needs to reach a consensus on the most likely causes and determine what data they need to test this conclusion. Do not discard the cause and effect diagram, it may well be that the causes you choose are not the root ones. Even if they are, then the diagram represents a large number of other potential causes and this is useful later when looking at ways of prevention rather than detection.

Activity 11.1

Choose a personal improvement target and draw up a statement for it, such as, 'doubling my income in twelve months' or 'getting an MBA within three years'. Now on a piece of A3 paper prepare a fishbone diagram of how to achieve your target. Include everything that will have to be overcome, every prerequisite. Identify as many different routes to achievement as you can and so on.

THEME ANALYSIS

During a brainstorming session a large number of ideas are generated in a random fashion. Theme analysis is a tool that enables some order to be brought to this list of ideas. The ideas are grouped under a series of headings or themes. The group agrees the themes and then works together to decide which theme each idea should be assigned to.

The starting point of a theme analysis is documenting the comments made. This involves transcribing the contents of flip-charts from the brainstorming sessions. No information is used which could be construed as interpreting other people's opinions. It is often easier to do the analysis using a computer with a spread-sheet that allows for several layers of sorting to occur at once.

The next stage is to sort the comments according to major themes. Often consistent ideas will already have been anticipated, for example, redundancies, relocation and foreign competition might all appear. Within each theme there might be further sub-themes. The material can be presented in many ways, although the most common is a series of pie charts illustrating the number of comments in each category.

Guidelines for theme analysis are as follows:

- Ideas are grouped into common themes.
- Avoid being too task-oriented.
- The group should agree the main themes.
- Aim for consensus.
- Allow sufficient time.

PARETO CHARTS

When you want to display the relative importance of numerical information about the probable causes of a problem, then the Pareto chart is a useful tool. A Pareto chart, named after the Italian economist who established the 80/20 principle, is a special form of vertical bar chart. Producing a Pareto chart from the data on tally sheets, check sheets or a theme analysis helps you to direct your attention and energy to the important issues rather than wasting time on trivia.

Select the factors that are going to be compared by brainstorming or by using existing data. Choose an appropriate standard unit for comparison – this could be frequency, but others such as annual cost or consequential loss might also be used. Agree the period that the team wants to compare across, such as a shift, eight hours or a week. Then gather the data before preparing the chart.

List the categories from left to right on the X or horizontal axis in the order of decreasing importance. Then draw a vertical bar on a scale determined by the unit of comparison. Often the Y or vertical axis is marked with the measurement scale used, but sometimes it is helpful to show a cumulative line as well so the axis may have to extend much higher. The value of the line is in answering questions such as 'How many of the causes account for 80 per cent of the problems?' Figure 11.2 illustrates a typical Pareto chart.

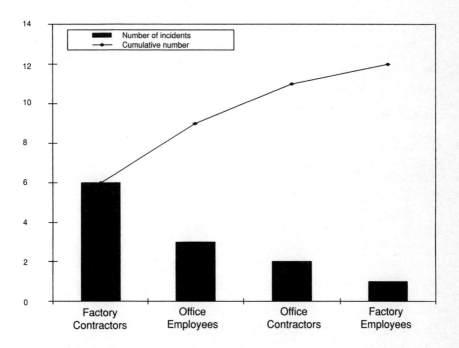

Figure 11.2 *Reported safety incidents (March 1999)*

SERVING FOLK

There is a small cluster of techniques based on word games and 'serving folk' is one of them. It takes its name from a Kipling poem:

> I keep six honest serving men,
> (They taught me all I know);
> Their names are What and Why and When
> And How and Where and Who.

This is a simple data structuring approach, especially useful for verifying that sufficient information has been obtained. The poem acts as a reminder to ask all six questions before proceeding. The technique is particularly popular with some journalists and especially junior reporters, whose articles can sometimes be seen to contain one paragraph on each question. Some people have developed this into a large-scale technique, although I prefer to keep it as a final cross-check.

In the grander form of serving folk, six flip-chart pages are prepared. One of the six words is put at the top of each sheet, and its opposite at the bottom:

What	What not
Where	Where not
Why	Why not
How	How not
When	When not
Who	Who not

The team can conduct a brainstorming session on the topic of 'Under what circumstances does the problem happen?' and can then transfer the items generated onto the six flip-charts in the appropriate places.

SWOT ANALYSIS

SWOT analysis – Strengths, Weaknesses, Opportunities, Threats – is a tool that has been popular in marketing organizations for some years, but has only recently begun to be used in problem solving. It is a data structuring approach. Many sources of data can be used, ranging from the output from brainstorming to the results of surveys and questionnaires, competitor analysis and bench-marking. The analysis can be written on flip-charts or an entire report can be structured to reflect the four categories represented by a combination of positive and negative influences operating internally and externally (see Figure 11.3). This approach can be adapted to a wide range of situations. It is popular with senior management teams as it allows them to consider both internal and external factors.

Figure 11.3 *SWOT analysis – the two dimensions*

Strengths

What is it about your company that represents its strengths in the market-place? These characteristics may not be unique but they are positive. Examples include size of parent company, lack of borrowing, existing presence in the market-place.

Weaknesses

Similarly, what does your company lack, or what are the characteristics that are not of help in the market-place? Examples are extent of borrowing, limited equity in directors' properties, image as a defence contractor.

Opportunities

What are the characteristics of the market-place that represent opportunities that you could exploit? For example, trend towards fixed price jobs, abundance of low quality one-man bands, expanding business expenditure.

Threats

What else is happening in the market-place that could prevent you from achieving what you want? For example, maturing technical knowledge in the market, lack of credibility for established names.

Activity 11.2

Why not carry out a SWOT analysis on yourself or your team at work? I often help people move from one job to another and find that the SWOT technique is very effective for helping them reposition themselves for job applications.

MODERATION TECHNIQUE

Moderation techniques of the kind described here originated in Germany for use with children with learning and behavioural difficulties. They were later seen to be of use with management teams and subsequently almost any kind of problem solving!

There are companies that sell proprietary products to support the technique including reference materials and training courses under the brand name 'Metaplan', but you can probably make do with some standard office stationery items! In the simplest form of the moderation technique, the room is prepared with large sheets of brown parcel wrapping paper (about 1 metre by 1.5 metres long) placed on the walls around it. A typical half-day session takes about six sheets. Participants are given small oblong cards about 10 centimetres by 7 centimetres and a felt-tipped pen. Post-it Notes of a similar size are even better.

The moderator leads the group and has a variety of other cards, including round ones, oblongs, and some with scales marked on them (commonly + 0 − or 0–10, see Figure 11.4), and also some glue. The easiest glue to use is the kind that comes in stick dispensers. The more colours to the Post-its and cards the better.

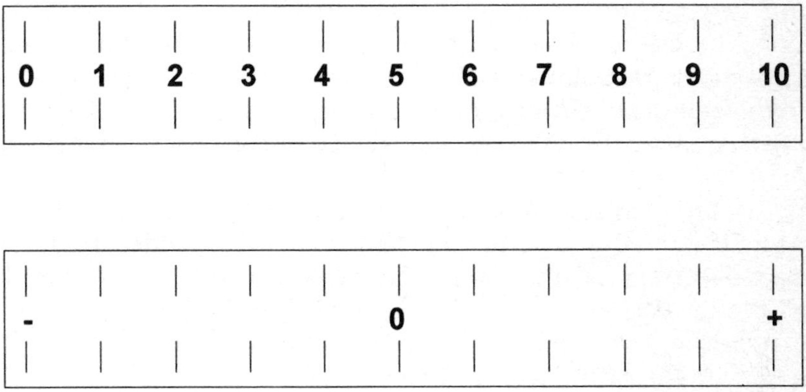

Figure 11.4

The session usually involves the group in quite an extensive period of preparation, especially if it is the first session that they have taken part in. Although the technique calls for team members to participate, and displays the results of their work in front of them at all times, it does not use the momentum effect that brainstorming generates. Instead, individuals can make their contributions without having to announce them in front of the whole team.

The moderator will begin by putting forward a proposition on a large oblong card on one of the sheets of brown paper. Some examples are:

- What are the qualities of an excellent operations group?
- What are the qualities of an excellent management consultancy?
- The characteristics of an excellent secretariat are...

The members of the team write as many ideas as they want on their small cards in large letters with only a couple of words on each card. After everyone has had a chance to write at least ten or twelve cards, the moderator asks them to come up and stick them to the brown paper (which is why Post-its save time).

When all the ideas are on the board the participants sit back and consider them. They are encouraged to add any more ideas that occur to them. The moderator will ask if anyone can spot themes. If so, these are written on large circles and placed at the top of fresh sheets of brown paper. The moderator, or an assistant, begins to assemble the individual cards underneath each theme, discussing the positioning with the team. Eventually all the cards are repositioned in columns and the moderator will draw a thick line around them with their title to keep them distinct.

Using a new sheet of brown paper, the moderator writes a large oblong for each of the themes that the group identified. These are placed in a column on the left of the sheet. On the right-hand side a scale from 0 to 10 on a long oblong is placed next to each theme. The team is then given small sticky dots about 1.5 centimetres in diameter of the kind that can be bought from most stationers. These dots represent votes and the members are told to put one on each scale to say how well they are achieving the factor described. This creates an immediate rush of activity and a clear visual impression of how the team feels.

Now the moderator poses the question, 'For each theme, how important do you think it is that we make changes soon?' To answer, each person is given a number of votes, usually the same number as there are themes. They have complete freedom to award their votes, placing them all on one theme if they think it is vital, or dividing them between the themes. Again, after a surge of activity this gives a clear visual impression of the priorities for change in the team.

The moderator may then focus attention on one theme, on a few, or continue to work in general terms, perhaps with a question such as, 'What are the factors that prevent us being an excellent... ?' Once more, ideas are written on cards and allocated to themes on brown paper sheets.

When the session comes to an end, there are a number of ways of enabling the participants to express their views about its value and how they would like to proceed. If appropriate the sheets can be photographed. I usually carry a small 35 millimetre camera and flash gun with me. It is perfectly satisfactory to take a black and white picture of each sheet where it is on the wall. The latest grain-less films can be processed at a High Street photo-lab and enlarged to 6 inches by 4 inches or 7 inches by 5 inches within a couple of hours. These prints can then be photocopied and distributed to the members of the team as a permanent record of the session.

Activity 11.3

Only one application of this powerful technique has been described; there are so many that it is difficult to know where to begin. If you have children, why not start with a domestic application? You can probably manage with a smaller-scale version using half a dozen sheets of flip-chart paper and some smaller square Post-its. Themes could include: 'An ideal summer holiday', 'Making enough pocket money', or 'The ideal house'. The possibilities are endless and if you can get the technique to work for a family with children, you will have no trouble at work!

AUTOMATED RECORDING

Tape recorders have been around for a long time but the technology continues to improve. Nowadays it is easy to buy a small tape recorder and set it up in a meeting to record the conversations. More on that in a moment, but for now consider some of the 'incidental' recording that happens in your organization. Modern computers, running Windows 3.1 and above keep some kind of log of what is happening at any time. Windows 98 has a tool called 'Outlook' that monitors files as they are saved, e-mails as they are sent, faxes as they are received and even letters as they are created and printed. There are all sorts of ways in which this information can be of use to a problem-solving team. At the network level there are similar tools and then the power for solving problems becomes incredible.

Many retail outlets, stores, banks, petrol stations, and so on, use video recording to survey a scene in case of crime. While these systems are notorious for not being maintained and the tapes being over-written, there are countless ways in which information like this can be used by a team. For example, one group in a regional airport recently had to improve the flow of passengers around the terminal building. They did so by examining speeded-up copies of the security videotapes. Another team working for a county council used the records from speed check cameras to estimate road movement and devise ways of preventing accidents in an adjacent housing estate. This latter have gone on to propose that the local Ambulance service use the same records to consider alternative routing for emergency vehicles at different times of the day.

Nowadays, many financial organizations provide telephone-based services. Their staff's conversations are recorded automatically. The information can be used in a number of ways though in practice it isn't always used in a particularly constructive one. For many this information is used more for policing the performance of the staff than for any creative purpose. However, one team in a bank recently used a random sample of recordings to prioritize the training of its staff. An insurance company used it to review the nature of their whole claims procedure as they had found too many forms were being sent out and either not completed at all or were incomplete.

Even seemingly simple systems often have a vast amount of information being accrued behind them. Ask yourself why the major supermarkets and petrol stations have invested so heavily in customer loyalty cards. Do you remember the days when all they did was give you little stamps to stick in a book? Of course today they can carry out extraordinary analyses of buying patterns and individual preferences. And again the data has enormous potential for problem-solving teams. Like the library that used the data from their automated borrowing system to plan staff rotas so that more specialist staff were available at certain times of the day when borrowers with particular interests tended to visit. The library was then able to offer seminars and special interest workshops to coincide. This not only brought in useful extra income but also improved overall usage of the facilities – usage that could be measured and presented to the management team that were responsible for providing funding.

VIDEO RECORDING

We've already mentioned the use of automated video recordings for data collection. It should go without saying that the use of a simple hand-held camcorder or similar device offers great potential to problem-solving groups. Placed statically they can capture all kinds of information about the movement of people in an organization. Moving around with them you can record all kinds of dynamic activities that would have gone unseen in the past. They are also great for recording historically. If you are about to introduce a change into an organization, walk around and record the scene beforehand. Even capture people's faces and expressions. Afterwards the video can have all kinds of merits but above all demonstrates one way or another the impact of the change that you have introduced.

Most modern PCs now have the facility to work with video images. You can buy a simple camera to attach to them and you can use this to capture basic images in suitable environments. Even when budgets are strictly limited, this kind of technology has become easily available. If you think it might be of help, then it's worth exploring further.

One further application that is worth mentioning is using the images captured and transmitting them either directly (if your company has the technology) or via the Internet (if it doesn't). In this way someone can be videoing something remotely and discussing it with their colleagues elsewhere. In the North Sea, for example, an engineer on an oil platform can walk around a seized drill or some other piece of apparatus with a video camera link-up and the images can be relayed direct to other engineers scattered around the world.

AUDIO RECORDING

While some recording happens unseen and unknown, you obviously have to act responsibly and check to see whether recording in the background is legally acceptable in your country. Often, though, the team will simply want to record a discussion, conversation or interview for review and some kind of analysis later. Simply ask – only once have I had someone object to this.

One extraordinary example of a problem-solving group using audio recording will demonstrate its potential. One morning in January 1994, I was on the platform of a railway in Tokyo. Sitting there was a glistening plain metal, full-scale model of a pre-production car from a well-known Japanese motor manufacturer. A few simple black-on-white signs placed around the car invited passers-by to inspect and 'play' with the car. The signs went on to say that spoken comments would be recorded by the engineers and used to improve the design before the vehicle went into commercial production. The car was smothered by passing Japanese businessmen. They were all talking excitedly. They chatted as they asked someone in the driving seat to release the bonnet. They chatted as they slammed it shut again. They chatted as they tried turning the steering and flicking the switches on the dash. The sunroof moved backwards and forwards as if it were on a continuous cycle as first one, then another besuited tester tried the novel transparent switch on the steering wheel. And so it went on. I can only guess how many were late for work that day! And all their comments were recorded through discretely placed microphones scattered around the vehicle. Over the coming weeks and months these comments would be scrutinized by the company engineers and genuinely used to hone the design.

The technology for audio recording has changed dramatically in recent years. Gone are the days of massive reel to reel recorders. Even the humble cassette recorder is now dated. While some radio broadcasters still use the Sony Professional Walkman they have mostly moved on to DAT recorders. The advantage of digital recorders is not only that the sound quality is better, which is obviously important for broadcasting, but also that they can be edited.

Whereas before, problem solvers usually had to transcribe the tape, it is now easier to edit the recording – cutting out long pauses, 'umms' and 'aahs' and long-winded explanations – to get to the real content. This can then be transcribed, or even used as sound-bites in a computer-based presentation such as Microsoft PowerPoint 97 and later allows you to attach edited clips to your slide! Today, DAT recorders cost little more than recording Walkman-style personal stereos.

Many businesses use hand-held dictation machines rather than the original music-cassette style of device. The latest generation of dictation systems takes this kind of approach to recording one step further. They use memory chips to record the sound. Typically 30 minutes of sound can be held on a chip. This is then edited on the machine before transferring to a PC that transcribes the text automatically with remarkable accuracy.

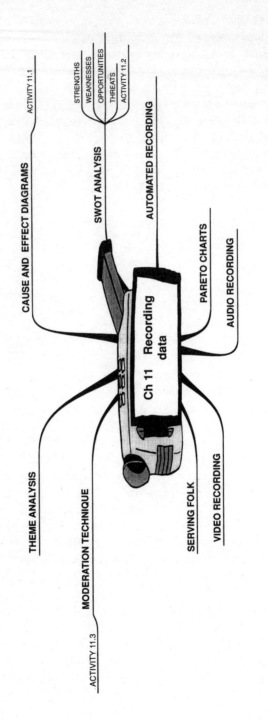

THEME ANALYSIS

MODERATION TECHNIQUE

ACTIVITY 11.3

SERVING FOLK

VIDEO RECORDING

CAUSE AND EFFECT DIAGRAMS

SWOT ANALYSIS

AUTOMATED RECORDING

PARETO CHARTS

AUDIO RECORDING

ACTIVITY 11.1

STRENGTHS
WEAKNESSES
OPPORTUNITIES
THREATS
ACTIVITY 11.2

Ch 11 Recording data

Figure 11.5 *Overview of Chapter 11*

CHAPTER 12

Informing ourselves and others

By now the team will have established its problem area and determined the priorities that need to be addressed. The purpose of the next stage is not only to gather information about potential solutions but also to explore those solutions in more depth.

One of the less overt objectives is for the team members to discuss the problem with a much wider audience. They may not actually meet people but they certainly need to gather their views. They may not carry out a formal survey but instead may involve other people in collecting data. If you review the section on the ORJI cycle in Chapter 4, you will realize that interviewers are not just collecting data, they are consciously transmitting something to the wider community and making a deliberate intervention. Skilful interviewers can not only gather important data for themselves, but also enhance the acceptability of their proposals. This may seem obvious, but even quite experienced managers often express frustration at the thought of yet another survey. It is for this reason that I prefer to use the phrase 'informing ourselves and others' rather than 'analysis'. This acts as a reminder of the dual role (and makes the PRIDE mnemonic work!).

This chapter is not intended to include every chart or diagram that it is possible to create, or every statistical test. It would be quite irresponsible for any team to base its recommendations on unsubstantiated, insignificant or irreproducible data provided, of course, that such information can be gleaned. In recent years the technology available has become far more sophisticated and even a comparatively basic desktop PC can perform statistical tests and graphic manipulations that were previously either the preserve of mainframe computers or the responsibility of highly skilled draughtspeople. Therefore the intention is merely to highlight a few techniques that might otherwise come to your attention and yet could save you an enormous amount of effort.

If you feel the need to read more about the basic tools, then as your first point of reference turn to the manuals that come with your computer software. For most purposes a straightforward spreadsheet will be perfectly adequate and the manuals and on-screen help facilities are often excellent.

One word of caution, however. To date there are very few expert systems acting as front-ends to computer software, and the old saying GIGO (garbage in, garbage out) still applies. This is particularly a problem with computer graphics packages, which will let you manipulate your data in hundreds of ways to produce the most aesthetically pleasing result. Unfortunately, this can also be the most misleading.

The simple illustration in Figure 12.1 should make the point. The lower illustration comes from an article in a management magazine. The article was trying to make a political point about falling employment. The second illustration shows the same data presented in an undistorted fashion.

DESIGNING SURVEYS

The preparation of surveys has three main elements. The first is the sampling pattern, the people you are going to ask. The second is the questionnaire, what you are going to ask them. The third is the interviewers and the preparation that they need.

As discussed above, the act of interviewing as well as more remote methods, is a form of intervention. If it is to be effective it has to be performed with some skill. Certainly if you were using outside consultants you would be very selective and would expect very well developed skills. It is important to maintain a similarly high level of skill in your own people.

Unfortunately you also want to maximize the contact between team members and their colleagues, and the two may not always seem compatible. If time permits, then at the very least the interviewers ought to have a training session to enhance their skills. If

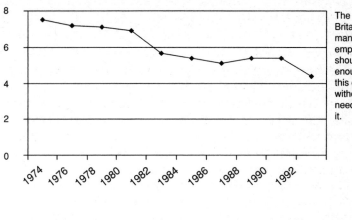

The downturn in Britain's manufacturing employment should be clear enough from this chart without the need to distort it.

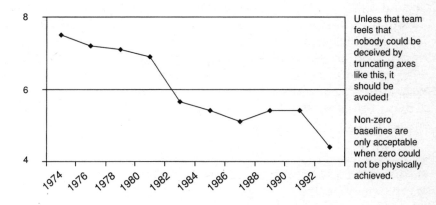

Unless that team feels that nobody could be deceived by truncating axes like this, it should be avoided!

Non-zero baselines are only acceptable when zero could not be physically achieved.

Figure 12.1   *Lies, damned lies and statistics*

not, then the team members should discuss the way that they will perform and perhaps try out a few sample interviews together.

EXPERIMENTAL DESIGN

Sometimes it is desirable to obtain the views of everybody in the company, or every customer, or every supplier. On other occasions this may not be required or resource limitations may mean that you want to solicit views from only a representative sample.

How do you find such a sample? There are many approaches, but one that is particularly good and yet rarely followed is to use an experimental design. One of the most efficient forms of experimental design is known as the 'fully saturated partial factorial design'. If that is too much of a mouthful try the Japanese equivalent, a 'Taguchi array'. The only difference is that Genichi Taguchi, a Japanese telecomm engineer, decided that if Japan waited for the statisticians to help every engineer and scientist in the aftermath of the Second World War it would take centuries for the country to recover. He produced some elegant little tables that anyone with a five-minute briefing could follow to perform incredibly complex experiments in a fraction of the time of traditional methods. While you can do a PhD in these topics this should not be necessary! A good training course will introduce you to many simple, yet sophisticated tricks and tips, but this section will give you the five-minute briefing which should be sufficient for all practical purposes. A practical example will be used which you can adapt.

Imagine that your team needs to establish what your customers think of the company and its products. You are a heavy engineering company with customers throughout Europe. You have been given very little time to carry out the study.

First, you need to draw up some simple lists. Begin with a list of the characteristics that distinguish your customers:

- location;
- distance for transport;
- volume of business with you;
- proportion of their business that they do with you;
- types of product that they order from you;
- how they use those products.

After brainstorming these characteristics, thin them down to a small number of particularly interesting comparisons, such as Southern European customers compared to UK ones, small order customers compared to major customers, and so on. You should aim for a set number of comparisons: 3, 7 or 15. Any more and the study will be too large. The cost and effort will be much less for three comparisons, but there will be no saving if you choose five rather than seven, so you might as well select seven and get more value out of the study. These comparisons are known as factors.

Now go to the accounts department and obtain a list of your

customers with the details that you have decided to investigate. Figure 12.2 comprises three arrays, one of which represents your experiment. Across the top are column letters, A, B, C, D, etc; each column corresponds to a factor. Down the left-hand side are numbers, 1, 2, 3, 4, etc; in this case they correspond to 'types of company', although they could correspond to types of employee, types of production run or whatever.

For 15 Factors

	A	B	C	D	E	F	G	H	I	J	K	L	M	N	O
1	0	0	0	0	0	0	0	0	0	0	0	0	0	0	0
2	0	0	0	0	0	0	0	1	1	1	1	1	1	1	1
3	0	0	0	1	1	1	1	0	0	0	0	1	1	1	1
4	0	0	0	1	1	1	1	1	1	1	1	0	0	0	0
5	0	1	1	0	0	1	1	0	0	1	1	0	0	1	1
6	0	1	1	0	0	1	1	1	1	0	0	1	1	0	0
7	0	1	1	1	1	0	0	0	0	1	1	1	1	0	0
8	0	1	1	1	1	0	0	1	1	0	0	0	0	1	1
9	1	0	1	0	1	0	1	0	1	0	1	0	1	0	1
10	1	0	1	0	1	0	1	1	0	1	0	1	0	1	0
11	1	0	1	1	0	1	0	0	1	0	1	1	0	1	0
12	1	0	1	1	0	1	0	1	0	1	0	0	1	0	1
13	1	1	0	0	1	1	0	0	1	1	0	0	1	0	0
14	1	1	0	0	1	1	0	1	0	0	1	1	0	1	1
15	1	1	0	1	0	0	1	0	1	1	0	1	0	1	1
16	1	1	0	1	0	0	1	1	0	0	1	0	1	0	0

For 7 Factors

	A	B	C	D	E	F	G
1	0	0	0	0	0	0	0
2	0	0	0	1	1	1	1
3	0	1	1	0	0	1	1
4	0	1	1	1	1	0	0
5	1	0	1	0	1	0	1
6	1	0	1	1	0	1	0
7	1	1	0	0	1	1	0
8	1	1	0	1	0	0	1

For 3 Factors

	A	B	C
1	0	0	0
2	0	1	1
3	1	0	1
4	1	1	0

Figure 12.2
Experimental design arrays

At the intersection of the columns and rows are numbers, but only 0 and 1. The numbers themselves are not significant, they are simply shorthand and are known as 'levels'. The 0 stands for one extreme and the 1 for the other extreme. You have to assign these levels to each factor. For the factor called order value, 1 means large and 0 means small. For the factor called location, 1 will mean mainland Europe and 0 will mean the United Kingdom. Finally, for the factor called product type, 0 will mean small syringes and 1 will mean big syringes.

Reading across the table for three factors indicates that your survey must include some companies that are based in the United Kingdom, placing small orders for small syringes – they are represented by the first row. The second group will include small order value, mainland European customers ordering large syringes. The third is UK-based, large order-value customers of large syringes and the fourth group orders large quantities of large syringes from mainland Europe.

Even though there are four more combinations of customers that are not being surveyed, you will be able to predict their opinion of you quite accurately. Halving the survey costs may not seem impressive, but when you are looking at seven factors the saving is nearly 94 per cent and on 15 factors it is 99.95 per cent. As this applies to almost any survey and does not affect its accuracy, it is worth exploring the possibilities! You might want to read a book about the original Japanese work,[1] or you might be interested in a book that places these techniques in the context of quality improvement teams.[2]

This technique has enabled you to identify specific groups of customers according to the factors that you are interested in. If you interview these customers you will be able to determine all that you need in order to answer your questions. But what are those questions?

DESIGNING QUESTIONNAIRES

Hundreds of questionnaires are circulated around the world every day. It is surprising how much junk mail is made up of questionnaires. Most of them are just seeking information for a sales database. Of those that are trying to find out your opinions – which is what you are concerned with in your survey – many of them cannot be rigorous. You can see this in the way that the questions are asked.

Compiling questionnaires is a complex subject and it is possible to write a whole book on the subject. If your team are considering questionnaires it is well worth getting a good book on the subject to glean examples of good practice.[3] This section will look at just two types of questions to see how they can be analysed.

Rank order questions

A common type of question that problem-solving groups are trying to answer is, 'Which of these solutions would be best for you?' This is because not all of them can be afforded or because they overlap in some way. You might decide to ask your customers the following:

Please would you rank the following possible product developments according to the benefit that you think they would bring to your company:

- smaller order volumes;
- straighter products;
- longer items;
- products with a better surface quality;
- shorter order lead times.

Mark the most important with 1, the next with 2 and so on.

You go to three separate companies meeting each of the types defined by your experimental design, that is 12 in total. The results of their rankings are shown in Table (a) in Figure 12.3. A quick glance suggests that there are some patterns in this but it is difficult to be precise and to say whether any differences are significant.

You begin by adding up the ranks for each item for each group of companies. The results are shown in Table (b). From now on you handle each factor that we are interested in separately. The illustration only follows the first one, one value, although the calculations are the same for all of them.

Now add the scores in the two columns that represent the lower level of the factor and do the same for the two columns that represent the upper level. Table (c) shows these figures together with the new rank order. Table (d) has exactly the same information but

Individual companies' responses

Factor												
A Order value	0			0			1			1		
B UK/Europe	0			1			0			1		
C Small/large syringes	0			1			1			0		
Ranked item												
Small order values	2	1	1	1	1	2	4	5	5	4	5	4
Straighter	5	5	4	5	4	5	3	2	3	5	4	5
Longer	4	4	5	4	3	3	2	1	1	3	2	1
Better surface	3	3	3	3	5	4	1	3	2	2	3	3
Shorter lead time	1	2	2	2	2	1	5	4	4	1	1	2

Sum of the ranks for each group of companies

Factor				
A Order value	0	0	1	1
B UK/Europe	0	1	0	1
C Small/large syringes	0	1	1	0
Ranked item				
Small order values	4	4	14	13
Straighter	14	14	8	14
Longer	13	10	4	6
Better surface	9	12	6	8
Shorter lead time	5	5	13	4

The rank of the sum of the ranks for each level

Factor				
A Order value	0		1	
Ranked item				
Small order values	8	1	27	5
Straighter	28	5	22	4
Longer	23	4	10	1
Better surface	21	3	14	2
Shorter lead time	10	2	17	3

The rank of the sum of the ranks for each level (rearranged in rank order for level 0)				
Factor A Order value	0		1	
Ranked item				
Small order values	8	1	27	5
Shorter lead time	10	2	17	3
Better surface	21	3	14	2
Longer	23	4	10	1
Straighter	28	5	22	4

Figure 12.3   *Analysing a rank order question*

rearranged so that the order of the items for one of the levels goes from 1 to 5.

If the companies that buy low order values have the same priorities as the ones that buy larger orders, then the rank orders will be the same. One measure of this similarity is the correlation coefficient. For ranked data there is a special version of this known as the Kendall rank correlation coefficient. It is very easy to calculate.

Look at the rank order for the second level. If it is close to the first level, the numbers will be in the right sequence. For the first number, 5, none of the following ones is in the right sequence and for each one we count -1. For the second number, 3, two are out of sequence but the last is correct. For the correct sequence we award +1. These numbers are allocated as follows:

First digit, 5	= −1	−1	−1	−1
Second digit, 3	= −1	−1	+1	
Third digit, 2	= −1	+1		
Fourth digit, 1	= +1			

The total score is −7 +3, or −4. In general terms, the maximum possible score is given by the formula:

$\frac{1}{2} \times n \times (n-1)$ where n is the number of items ranked. In this case it is $\frac{1}{2} \times 5 \times (5-1)$, or 10.

The correlation coefficient is the ratio of the actual score to the maximum possible. In this case it is −0.4: the two sequences are negatively correlated. Table 12.1 shows the probability of obtaining a particular score by chance (S) according to the number of items ranked (N). You will see that in the case discussed there is a probability of 0.24. This means that if the two groups were ranking the items identically there is only a 24 per cent chance of obtaining a score of 4.

Table 12.1   *Probabilities for the Kendall correlation coefficient*

Number of items ranked (N)

Score

(S)	4	5	6	7	8	9	10
0	63	59	–	–	55	54	–
1	–	–	50	50	–	–	50
2	38	41	–	–	45	46	–
3	–	–	36	39	–	–	43
4	17	24	–	–	36	38	–
5	–	–	24	28	–	–	36
6	4	12	–	–	27	31	–
7	–	–	14	19	–	–	30
8	–	4	–	–	20	24	–
9	–	–	7	12	–	–	24
10	–	1	–	–	14	18	–
11	–	–	3	7	–	–	19
12	–	–	–	–	9	13	–
13	–	–	1	4	–	–	15
14	–	–	–	–	5	9	–
15	–	–	–	2	–	–	11
16	–	–	–	–	3	6	–
17	–	–	–	1	–	–	8
18	–	–	–	–	2	4	–
19	–	–	–	–	–	–	5
20	–	–	–	–	1	2	–

Most statisticians would say that this is not sufficiently remote to describe it as statistically significant – it would need to be around 0.05 to be this. Most problem-solving groups would say that the statisticians were over-cautious!

Activity 12.1

Now attempt an analysis of one of the other factors. If you find that there is a tie between items for the rank, split the difference, thus two items tying for third place will both be given a rank of 3.5.

Yes/No choices

In the same survey you decide to ask people how you compare with your competitors. You do so with the following question:

For each of the following, please say whether we are the best of your suppliers or not (ring one):

- Accuracy of orders   Best   Not best
- Completeness of documentation   Best   Not best
- Meeting target delivery times   Best   Not best

The responses are shown in Figure 12.4.

Individual companies' responses												
Factor												
A Order value	0			0			1			1		
B UK/Europe	0			1			0			1		
C Small/large syringes	0			1			1			0		
Yes/No item												
Documentation	W	W	W	B	B	B	B	B	W	W	B	W
Delivery times	B	W	W	B	B	B	B	B	W	W	W	W

Contingency table for documentation			
Factor C Small/large syringes	Large	Small	Total
Better than the rest	A 5	B 1	E 6
Worse than some	C 1	D 5	F 6
Total	G 6	H 6	K 12

Figure 12.4 *Analysing a yes/no question*

You will notice that the results for each company are very different. Of course, it is unlikely always to be so obvious. You can use what is known as the Fisher exact probability test to find out whether the differences are significant.

Statisticians have a clever symbol known affectionately as the 'shriek'. It is usually represented by a '!' and it stands for the factorial of a number. The factorial of a number is the product of all whole numbers from that number down to 1. Thus the factorial of 5, written 5!, is 5 x 4 x 3 x 2 x 1, or 120.

Using the same letters as shown in the figure, the exact probability of obtaining a particular set of frequencies in a 2 x 2 contingency table is:

[(E!.F!.G!.H!) / (K!.A!.B!.C!.D!)]

In this case it is:

[(6!.6!.6!.6!) / (12!.5!.1!.1!.5!)]

Which you can work out to be:

[(720 × 720 × 720 × 720) / (479001600 × 120 × 120)]

or

[(26.873856 × 10^10) / (689.762304 × 10^10)]

or

0.156.

These look gruesome calculations, but of course the power of the PC makes them straightforward.

Even the statistician who invented this test considered that the arithmetic was too much! If you want to avoid carrying this out you can buy tables for most circumstances. There are two excellent books on this type of statistics, which are constantly being reprinted.[4]

Activity 12.2

Now try one of the other factors.

RUN CHARTS

The basic run chart was described in Chapter 10, which also explained how to turn it into a statistical process control (SPC) chart if necessary. When samples of data are taken from a large population they have a most frequently occurring value (mode) that is about the mid-point of their range. With half the values below it and half above it, it is also the average and the median. Do not worry if you are unfamiliar with this terminology; what you do need to be aware of is that sometimes the symmetrical curve associated with these samples changes shape.

DISTRIBUTIONS

The pattern of a distribution like that described above can be useful for interpreting what is going wrong. Often groups spend a long time investigating the wrong area because they did not look at the distribution first. First, prepare a histogram of the data. Equipped with this you can begin to interpret what is happening. Figure 12.5 illustrates various distribution patterns.

As you can see, the different shapes produced reflect different distortions of the data. On the left-hand side are two very common problems. In the first case (a) the samples that have been collected have incorporated two distinct populations. As a result, any basic statistical manipulation applied to them, such as averages and standard deviations, will be meaningless.

The second picture (b) is of a skewed distribution. This may mean that the population itself is distorted, although this is relatively unusual. Alternatively the data could be moving in the direction of the skew through time, in other words the mean is shifting. In this case a run chart should be produced and the team needs to look for the cause of the drifting mean.

On the right-hand side are two examples (c) and (d) that are particularly common in organizations that employ inspection-

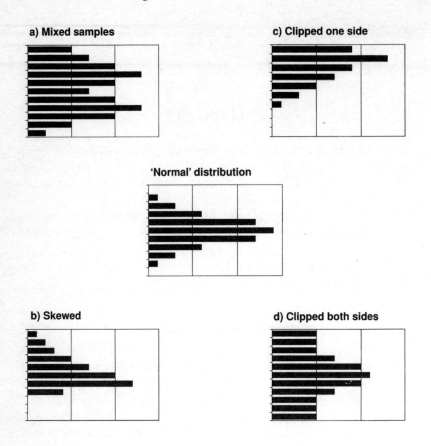

Figure 12.5   *Diagnosing problems from a distribution*

based quality methods. In the top example the production process mean is very close to the lower limit of tolerance, perhaps for cost purposes. Someone has implemented a control to eliminate items that fall outside the limit. This is always a very costly approach and can never be totally effective.

The distribution that is clipped both sides is, at least, targeted properly, but there is so much variation that the product is being screened at both the upper and lower limits. This is typical of distributions for products that are graded mechanically according to size.

STEM AND LEAF DIAGRAMS

One effective tool for testing both the time-based distribution and the overall sample distribution is the 'stem and leaf' diagram (see Figure 12.6). This is simply a horizontal histogram of the kind illustrated in the previous examples but pointing in the opposite direction, so that its X axis is the same as the Y axis of a run chart pointing in the usual direction. The two use the same X axis but different Y axes. The 'leaves' are tally marks added as the run chart is built up.

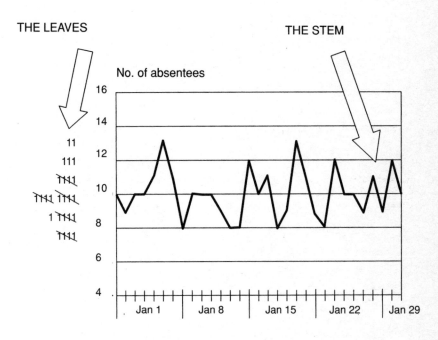

Figure 12.6   *Stem and leaf diagram*

Many statistical tasks assume that the data is normally distributed, that is it has a characteristic bell-shaped distribution. Rather than resort to complicated mathematics, plotting the stem and leaf diagram allows us to check the shape visually.

NOTES

1 Taguchi, G (1986) *Introduction to Quality Engineering*, Asian Productivity Organization, via UNIPUB, New York

2 Wilson, G B (1993) *On Route to Perfection*, IFS, Bedford

3 Oppenheim, A N (1966) *Questionnaire Design and Attitude Measurement*, Heinemann, London

4 Siegel, S (1956) *Nonparametric Statistics for the Behavioural Sciences*, McGraw-Hill, London; and Kendall, M (1975) *Rank Correlation Methods*, Griffin, High Wycombe

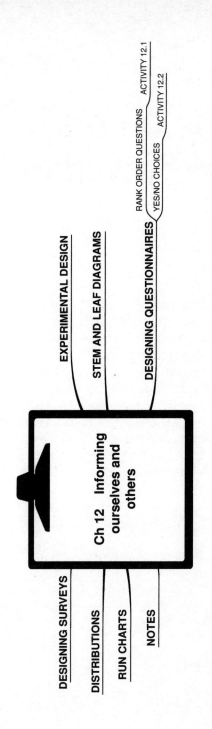

DESIGNING SURVEYS

DISTRIBUTIONS

RUN CHARTS

NOTES

Ch 12   Informing ourselves and others

EXPERIMENTAL DESIGN

STEM AND LEAF DIAGRAMS

DESIGNING QUESTIONNAIRES

RANK ORDER QUESTIONS   ACTIVITY 12.1

YES/NO CHOICES   ACTIVITY 12.2

Figure 12.7   *Overview of Chapter 12*

CHAPTER 13

Deciding on and designing solutions

There's a well-known analogy that the man who designed the world's greatest mouse trap died penniless because no one came and bought it. 3M's Post-it Notes were many years in the making, not because the product wasn't ready to go, but because no one had demonstrated that it could be marketed (after all who would want to buy some off-cuts of paper with a glue that didn't stick properly?). The problem-solving team has exactly the same problem. They don't only need to identify the solution, but they need to think carefully how they are going to implement it. Even then, they usually need to go to someone to get approval so they have to sell their solution and its implementation plan.

DESIGNING SOLUTIONS

There are three techniques that probably have their greatest merit at this stage. It is also worth considering others too. For example, you may want to try implementing a pilot solution and measure its effect; if so, the Taguchi techniques described in the previous chapter could be invaluable.

Solution by analogy

Investigating a solution by analogy enables the team to think creatively while concentrating on identifying solutions to specific problems. Having collected information about the problem, the team members create a display of relevant facts. They then list, possibly through brainstorming, other situations analogous to their own.

Suppose that a team has identified a problem with scheduling. Rather like modern approaches to benchmarking, the team then identifies other organizations that must have similar problems and tries to say how they handle their situation. In benchmarking the analysis is considerably deeper, but here the benefit comes from quick insights rather than profound thought. Some groups find that this approach is particularly successful. Teams that share a wide range of experience are usually quick to throw light on old problems.

> ## Activity 13.1
>
> Try this technique on a business activity on which you spend a lot of time, for example writing reports or attending meetings. Create a list of other organizations that you imagine must hold even more meetings and write even more reports. With this in front of you, create a list of the ways in which you think they must do things to achieve their results. Could you use or adapt any of these methods?
>
> Now draw a line across both pages. Add to the first list people who perform analogous activities. For instance, if the list is about report writing some analogies might be month end accounts, flight logs, delivery schedules or warehouse inventories. Build up the second list with the ways that you imagine these are carried out. Are there any ideas that you could use here?

Force field analysis

At a given moment there are forces acting on almost everything. Most situations to do with work can be envisaged as having two sets of forces – those that encourage the situation and those that prevent or discourage it. Problem solving is often concerned with shifting the balance. For example, if your problem involves late deliveries there will be some forces that encourage earlier deliveries. If you have reached a stable situation where deliveries are not getting better or worse, then there must be restraining forces that are preventing matters from improving any further.

The team members begin by defining the scale along which you are trying to improve. They record where you are, where you are coming from and where you are going to. It can add a little interest if the scale is recorded on strips of paper across a wall. If the team has a dedicated room this can be left up as a permanent record and to monitor improvements as they are achieved.

Divide the area above the scale into three parts. On the left prepare a list of the forces that you can identify that are preventing improvement. On the right prepare a similar list of the forces encouraging improvements. Divide the middle area into four columns. Head the left-hand column 'importance', the next 'influence', then 'urgency' and finally 'price'. This is illustrated in Figure 13.1.

Preventing improvement	Importance	Influence	Urgency	Price	Encouraging improvement
Scale for improvement					

Figure 13.1   *Force field analysis*

Try to establish the weight of each force, that is, how much influence is being wielded by that force. Sometimes, especially in manufacturing problems, this can be identified quite accurately, especially if the team has carried out a number of designed experiments and determined the impact of the various factors. In non-manufacturing problems it is often easier to rank the forces rather than trying to attach an absolute scale to them. The group now rates the forces in the four columns, usually with a simple code (A, B, C; a, b, c; i, ii, iii or similar).

The team has now established all the information that is needed to allocate priorities in the implementation plan. Solutions that tackle major forces should take priority over those that do not. The higher the rating in the central area the higher the priority – except 'price'!

Originally people using force field analysis were encouraged to emphasize the removal of restraining forces rather than adopting an overpowering strategy. Nowadays, the harsh economic reality can sometimes mean that teams are left with little choice than to adopt this route, but the philosophy is still valid.

CASE STUDY 13.1

BAA has a role as construction contractor for the fifth terminal at London's Heathrow Airport. The construction of the terminal would have begun a lot sooner – with benefits all round – if BAA had been able to offer compensation to those who opposed the planning application. Instead the company and the complainants are forced to go through hearings, inquiries and the courts in a confrontational way, all of which costs both parties a great deal. This is a straightforward instance where removing the restraining forces would be better than wasting effort trying to overpower them, but our legal system does not allow it.

Force field analysis is a good tool for organizations with a strong analytical bent. It is also a useful approach when preparing for a presentation to senior management. Faced with the information it elicits, senior managers will find it difficult to deny that the group has got to grips with the problem and thought of all the consequences of the solution.

Systems design

Most large organizations have information technology (IT) specialists. Their role usually involves a combination of maintenance, operations and systems design. Many of the tools for systems design were developed in the days before the widespread application of PCs and are really suited to large-scale solutions. It will be interesting to see which alternatives emerge as the organization of the future demands an approach more suited to small teams operating independently and possibly even commercially separate. As the largest purchaser of IT services at the time, in 1980 and 1981 the Ministry of Defence established certain standards for systems analysis.

Both systems analysis and design can be carried out without resorting to an IT solution. Many teams find themselves in the position of redesigning processes and they need to understand the skills of systems analysis and design.

It is very easy for an individual to take over the systems analysis activity. For someone who likes structures, logic and detail, the diagrams involved and the analysis are *fun*. However, it has been discussed before why it is so important for teams to be involved – please don't forget!

Entity models

There are many similarities between models of systems analysis and problem solving, but it is in the convergent phase of structured approaches that the most useful exchange takes place. Most contemporary methods are based on the information or data that is handled. They define basic chunks of information or 'entities' that may relate to one another but are nevertheless discrete. Examples include product specifications, production schedules or quality assurance (QA) sample records. Each is a comprehensive set of information on its own but there are also interrelationships between them. Most of these entities have what is known as a 'one to many' relationship with the others, thus one product specification is related to many QA samples. Not all entities will have a relationship with all others. The exact nature of the relationships depends on the business processes.

One of the tools of systems analysis is an 'entity model' of the data within a business process. This shows the real connections between the different types of information according to how they are used. Often preparing such a diagram highlights redundant information flows, where the data would go from A to C through B, and therefore does not need to pass directly from A to C as well. In the example in Figure 13.2 there is a redundant flow from the production plan to the production schedule, as the same information is available from the sales ledger. Redundant flows often tie up resources, both in terms of people and paperwork. The team will probably consider removing them entirely from the new process.

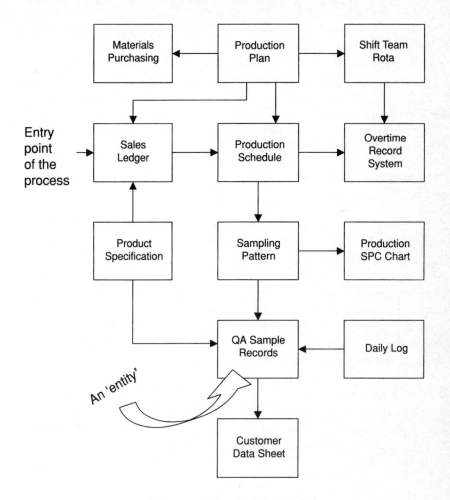

Figure 13.2   *Entity model*

Data flow diagrams

The entity model shows how some information is related to other information; it does not show how the process itself flows. This is a subtle but important distinction. Which activities change the data? How do you make sure that each part of the process has up-to-date information?

Such aspects are revealed in a data flow diagram. There is a more complex set of items to show, but these diagrams usually relate more to the physical world. Figure 13.3 is a data flow diagram for the same processes as used in the entity model, and includes most of the symbols commonly employed. The closed rectangles are processes. The open-ended rectangles are stores of information; no processing happens here but different processes can draw on the information from the same store. The ovals are external activities that feed into the present one but are not included in any detail.

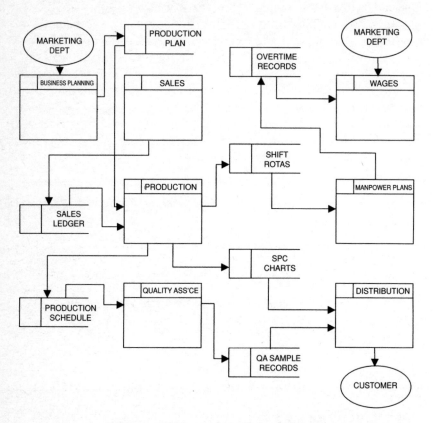

Figure 13.3   *A data flow diagram*

For each process (ie each rectangle) a more detailed diagram using exactly the same symbols may be prepared. This progressive 'zooming in' allows highly complex processes to be portrayed in sufficient detail.

Once more the team members will be trying to identify redundant processes, duplicated storage of information, unnecessary activities and so on. They will also identify cases where information ought to be available but the system does not provide it. A very common example is the lack of historical information available when internal budgets are set.

The examples given here show the situation within a traditional, functionally organized operation. Recently, information-handling software has undergone a revolution. First, free-form databases emerged allowing users to store their information in much less structured ways. The multi-view/multi-source software was developed. This allows people to examine and combine data from a very wide range of sources. Operating on local networks, accessing corporate systems, and automatically scanning the Internet, people can develop reports from diverse and less integrated sources. Finally, the technology to distribute these 'reports' has been incorporated into the Web standard, HTML, so that independently developed systems can readily exchange data. This approach provides the communication flows between processes that previously required human effort to sustain them.

Activity 13.2

Use the systems analysis tools to illustrate a process with which you are familiar. You might choose one of the activities in which you are involved at work. Alternatively, a charity or community organization might provide some useful insights. Two delegates on courses that I ran produced fascinating analyses: one of the local planning process and the other of the registration process for MBA students. In both cases they highlighted some excellent opportunities for improvement!

Activity 13.3

Look again at the two diagrams of the production system. Try to redraw them as they might evolve over the next few years.

Control analysis

You might ask why control is being discussed when the trend is towards empowering people. Many organizations have rigid systems to ensure that more senior people are involved in decision-making according to the perceived risk. The commonest example is spending authority. Mortals can spend £5 while chief executives can spend millions, and so on. Often such controls are not as rigidly applied to non-financial risks – any mortal can open a sluice and poison the local stream, for instance – even though the cost to the company may be very high in both fines and bad PR. Obviously it would be impractical for every action that could conceivably cause a problem to be referred up through the organization. Nevertheless, traditional books on systems design talk of authorization, accountability and approval. They make use of audits, segregation of duties, supervision and review.

Such methods are no longer considered good management practice; indeed companies are spending a fortune trying to rid themselves of these approaches that create a culture of distrust, seniority and positional power. This is why teams need to think of alternatives when they are designing new ways of working. Ideally the new way should be preventative, that is, prevent the process from continuing until everything is satisfactory.

The extent to which the team thinks of alternatives will depend on how critical the process is. It needs to make an assessment, looking at the way the system is used, what it produces, how the output is used, and what could go wrong. This is known as criticality analysis. Typical problems with output, for example, include accidental loss, and information becoming corrupted or incomplete. In the past, books placed a lot of emphasis on dishonesty, theft and deliberate falsification – today we prefer to trust people!

Activity 13.4

Take the design that you produced (Activity 13.3) for a team-based production process. Rule a large sheet of paper, in landscape format, into three columns. In the left-hand column, assess the system for possible problems. What problems could occur? What impact would they have? Order the problems in terms of decreasing severity.

In the middle column, describe how and where the problems would reveal themselves, and if this differs from where they might actually occur. Assess each for probability. Reorder the items so that critical and high probability issues are at the top of the list and less critical and low probability items are at the bottom.

In the right-hand column, identify preventative controls for each issue. If you can't think of preventative measures, then try to invent ways in which the system can correct itself or finally resort to detection methods.

SELLING TO SENIOR MANAGEMENT

At some stage in almost any problem-solving process, no matter how large or small, those responsible for deciding on the solution and designing it, must sell their ideas to others, especially to the holders of power in the organization, typically the senior managers.

Advertising and sales people have a simple but highly effective approach to achieving this and we can learn from it, called AICDC (Attention, Interest, Conviction, Desire and Close) Nowadays, the same model is used to structure presentations of all kinds where we are asking our audience to take action, not just to part company with their cash!

Attention

THIS COULD BE THE MOST VALUABLE FIVE MINUTES IN YOUR LIFE... . And that isn't so extreme either. After all, the best possible solution is pretty useless if no one buys in to it. To get our message across we need to grab our potential buyers' attention.

Interest

How do you define 'management'? And what about 'leadership'? There's a little known fact that as much as 80 per cent of senior management time is spent sorting out other people's problems. Empirically, that is another way of defining management. It seems that in most organizations the managers' efforts get diverted into helping sort out things that other people could, should and would like to deal with themselves, but for some reason they can't. In some ways this whole book is about trying to help them do so and certainly your solution should be.

Conviction

Far better for the solution that we are proposing to be put into place, for the managers to no longer get sucked into problem solving and instead focus their attention on real leadership. Real leadership means having real impact; it makes a difference in the long term and in big ways to the bottom line too. It is far more satisfying than simple day-to-day fixing things up.

Desire

So which would you rather do? Be a manager or be a leader? Does it make sense to have a real feeling of achievement each day? Would you like to retire knowing that you have really made a difference to the world around you? Would you like your part of the business to excel? To be seen as the source of best practice not only here but maybe throughout the whole company? Or even in the industry as a whole?

Close

Well, seriously – all you need to do is read this book, apply its messages in a sensible, practical way and with thought, and all this could be yours!

Applying AICDC

Next time you have to write a letter that calls for action, or make a presentation, or run a workshop or seminar, or issue a new document, give some thought to the AICDC model and structure your work that way. You'll find that there are even templates now available for this model within some of the computer-based presentation packages like Microsoft PowerPoint.

INTRODUCING CHANGE

Implementing a solution to a problem is just as difficult as finding it in the first place. We are trying to change the way in which people behave and in order to do so they have to give up the way they have been behaving in the past. Even an apparently simple change, such as introducing a new form, can provoke all kinds of reaction – and not always the one we were expecting.

Obviously, there are differences according to scale but the process that you need to go through and the elements that need to be considered are the same, whether it's a simple procedural change, a wholesale restructuring or a deliberate attempt to change the culture of the business.

CASE STUDY 13.2

A good example is the recent introduction of a new EPOS (electronic point of sale) system into a chain of dry cleaners. To achieve a smooth transition, the team knew that they would have to provide basic training in the use of the new till. Their plan focused almost entirely on this aspect. Fortunately, a member of the regional management team recognized what was likely to happen and intervened. A process of internal marketing was developed, using powerful arguments about the business advantages of the new system, drawing staff attention to their competitors and how they were operating a similar, newer system. Training was linked to an incentive – people attending the training were given vouchers for members of their family to use the many other services offered by the chain. The training was developed by sales trainers rather than the IT professionals – linked to how to get more sales and, with a computer-simulation as part of the programme, the staff found the training more relevant and potentially lucrative to them through their branch bonus scheme. The implementation was carried out in a staggered fashion, so that the area managers could be present in each branch for the first couple of days. In the first week of operation in a branch the staff all met at the end of the day to discuss the new system and any ideas they had about working with it. They were given a 'hotline' to call to discuss any ideas that they wanted to share and in this way a priority list for a subsequent update to the system was developed. As a consequence, not only was the implementation achieved in a smoother fashion, but it produced a positive effect on sales whereas the original team had predicted an initial downturn as the staff got to grips with the new equipment.

Almost any change in the way people behave can lead to a change in the culture of the organization. In some cases this will be quite small and local, while in others it can be massive and directed. In the following section we are going to look at the change towards a different culture. If you really believe that the change that you are implementing is a minor one, then you will probably want to simplify the steps but do so sensitively as it is easy to underestimate the effort needed.

Why change culture?

To anyone who has not been involved in culture change, the very idea that it is possible may seem remarkable. In the past, many people worked for the same organization from their apprenticeship at 15 to retirement at 65. Today the trend is towards shorter, even fixed-term, appointments of one, two or three years. While this has advantages and disadvantages, one positive aspect is the richness of experience that people acquire. People have different views about how quickly culture change can occur. They often say that culture is one of the most durable aspects of an organization and can outlast any employee. Most organization development specialists will be able to give examples of senior managers who have tried to introduce change only to find themselves out of a job six months later. On the other hand, some people say that it is possible to change the culture systematically, provided that you win the cooperation of senior managers. Again, most of us can give examples of a new manager who has had a dramatic effect on the way a department behaves.

The managers in organizations undergoing culture change have a vital role to play. They will enable it to happen.

Successful change in organizations

Changes in corporate culture are attempted for a variety of reasons. There is usually (although not exclusively) a perception that something could be better than it currently is. Formal culture changes in recent years have tended to concentrate on a few areas, within which there is considerable overlap:

- customer focus;
- quality and productivity improvement;
- safety;
- leadership;
- innovation;
- environment;
- society focus.

Changes in the public sector have also involved these areas, although many have been associated with a different philosophy following changes in higher levels of organization and funding. The sectors affected have included:

■ railways;
■ hospitals;
■ general medical practices;
■ police forces;
■ the armed forces;
■ schools;
■ universities;
■ airports and aviation.

So far, in the United Kingdom, the one area that has not been dramatically revised is that of local government, but a trend has been set by the creation of assemblies for Scotland and Wales recently.

In almost every setting there are internal or external 'experts' who claim to have developed the definitive approach to changing culture. Simple, single case, experiential models of this kind are only really useful if the environment in which they are applied is the same. What works for Nissan would not work for Ford or Toyota. Circumstances vary greatly, and unfortunately the more sophisticated the tool or technique, the less likely it is to translate successfully from one environment to another.

Grieving process

While the process of change varies greatly, there are some aspects of change that are almost universal. This is because they are related more to the reactions of people than to the mechanics of the change itself. One of these was alluded to earlier. The individuals are being asked to give up practices, relationships, attitudes and sometimes even emotions that they have grown so accustomed to that it is difficult to acknowledge that there are others. Being told that the way you have been working for 20 years is no longer the best provokes strong reactions in all of us. The response of many people is similar and is illustrated in Figure 13.4.

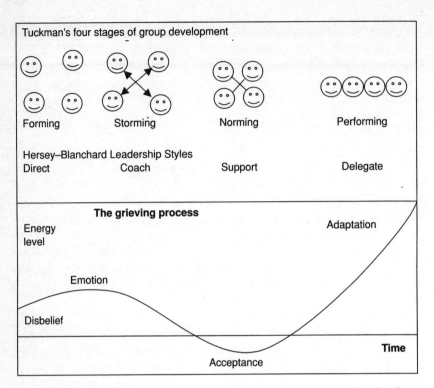

Figure 13.4   *Emotional responses in teams and individuals*

Disbelief

The first reaction that we all have to loss is to deny it. With the loss of a loved one, relatives will often comment that an individual doesn't really seem to have come to terms with their loss. At a very simple level, when introducing a new working practice in an organization you will hear people say, 'I don't believe it!'

Emotion

We then show our emotion. We may cry or become angry; we may shout and scream; be sarcastic to our colleagues; make snide remarks within hearing of our managers. Even if people don't demonstrate their emotions at work, as it seems to be a strongly held taboo in some organizations, then they will often find an outlet for them elsewhere – perhaps a drinking session with friends, or a shopping spree at the weekend, or perhaps by taking it out on their partner at home. In recent years, I have separated mature directors who had grabbed one another by the lapels over a boardroom table, seen supervisors fighting one another in the car park and listened to seasoned managers crying over a difficult decision. If you deny that this happens in the 'real' world ask your spouse if you have ever gone home in the evening and displayed your pent-up emotions!

Acceptance
After the storm, the lull! We enter a low energy phase; a time where we collect our thoughts; where we really appreciate the impact of what has happened and what it means to us. People are left feeling drained. This sounds all negative, but it needn't be. Even after major industrial relations breakdowns, where the anger has been demonstrated violently, in the aftermath people can stop, reflect and see that some of the assumptions and fears were unfounded. It is only really now that we are accepting that the change has happened.

Adaptation
And so we adapt: our work to the new culture; our relationships to the new team; our family to our new working pattern; and so on. The process of adaptation can happen surprisingly quickly in some individuals and more slowly in others. This can be a source of frustration, especially to those that were aware of the change beforehand, and so it is important to allow time for our colleagues to adapt too. There is something that you can do to help people as they work through these stages.

Leadership style

In recent years there has been a lot of research into management behaviour. Many earlier textbooks prescribed a single style: firm, yet available, with clear boundaries of what could and couldn't be done. Today, thankfully, we are a little more enlightened though it has taken a long time to percolate from the researchers to becoming real practice especially at the more senior levels of organizations. Fortunately as much of the wealth of countries today is tied to smaller and younger businesses the shift in approach is happening.

The relevance of this research here lies in its connection to people's emotional state. The work of Ken Blanchard and Paul

Hersey is typical of this new approach and ties nicely to the stages of the grieving process described above.[1, 2, 3] They describe four styles of leadership that may be switched between by someone as they work with another person's different emotional states. Taken as a whole the sequence illustrated in Figure 13.5 charts the route you would also take as you develop someone's skills to perform a specific task, or fulfil a particular role.

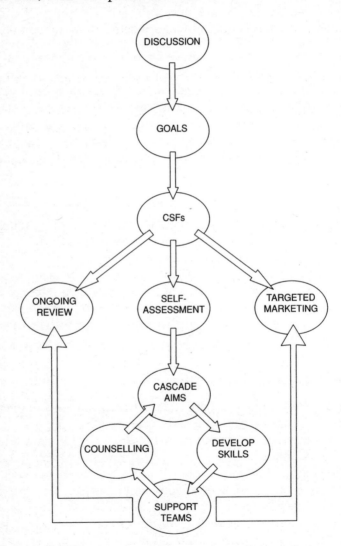

Figure 13.5   *Successful change in organizations*

Direct
Without being too blunt, the individual who is in 'disbelief' needs the facts reinforcing. This is a directing style. Confronted instead with an amorphous sponge which absorbs their concerns but offers nothing tangible in return the individual is going to find out what has happened in their own way, is more likely to jump to conclusions and react accordingly. It is at times like this that clear statements, given in a non-concealing fashion, even if they are statements of what is not known, are better than 'no comment'.

Coach
In the emotional stage, people still need real answers but they also want a supportive and understanding approach. Termed coaching this is similar to the stance of a high school sports coach – acting almost as a surrogate parent. The balance between giving information and providing support is a difficult one to achieve and this is probably the skill that most managers have the toughest time learning.

Support
In their drained state, people need support. They are not ready to act yet, and do not respond well to 'gung ho' managers trying to stimulate productivity artificially. Without becoming a perpetual shoulder to cry on the managers need to take on a listening style and not directing.

Delegate
As momentum builds up again, productivity naturally increases, people take on board the change and adapt to it. The leader's job is largely complete. This is the time to delegate, letting people get on with the task themselves. Of course this doesn't mean forgetting about them – to delegate effectively you still have to keep in touch.

Some time ago, Tuckman described four stages that groups go through when they are becoming a team. These too map onto the same continuum.

Forming is the process by which they get to know one another. You will often see groups going through this phase with the individuals behaving as they usually would when mildly unsure of themselves. Some people will hold back, others will be very extrovert, others will try to entertain the group and so on.

Storming follows with certain members of the group demonstrating their frustration with other members. There is a temptation to only see this as one individual or another not fitting in. In practice, the individual who attracts the group's anger is only a scapegoat and they are really venting their frustrations at one another.

Norming is about developing ground rules. It is fascinating seeing this happen. It can be done in a very straightforward way or less obviously. One internet discussion group spent nearly a month, after four months of meeting, discussing how they would run their meetings. Often a member will try to suggest some rules by which they can run more 'effectively'. Sometimes these rules are useful, others are not and some are just an attempt to paper over the cracks without really storming properly.

Performing is the end result. The group have got to know one another, catharticaly shared some emotions together, and agreed how they are going to work together. Now they can get on with whatever they are there for.

Making change happen[4]

Over the last few years we have worked with many organizations in various states of change and collected extensive case studies of successful change. From these experiences we have tried to identify the key facets of any such process. We do not pretend that this is the definitive approach, but we do believe that each element is sufficiently important that it should be considered carefully in the planning of any change initiative. The full set is illustrated in Figure 13.5.

Discussion

For most organizations that are about to embark on a change process, one of the first steps is for their senior managers to spend time reviewing strategies and exploring alternatives. This process may involve 'away days', seminars and conferences, and circulating relevant literature. The events may be initiated by the parent company, by a local director or general manager, or by the industry representative body and they can be organized by almost anybody. The content of this kind of event is usually much less important than the fact that the people attending are surrounded by like-minded peers. This reinforces the idea that it is acceptable to be challenging and questioning.

There are many ways of encouraging people to take part in the process and benefit from their explorations. The top team may hold extensive debriefings after each event, or they may not discuss together what took place at all. We often find that three people travelling together have a very fruitful debrief on the way home! The discussion stage is very important since without it people can feel steamrollered into the change and may react negatively.

Clarifying the goals

The next stage in the process is to reach a common understanding of what the new culture means and how it relates to your organization. You will need to reach a consensus on your vision for the business and will probably identify some of the implications of not going down this route. You will agree about where you are now and where you want to be. Most importantly you will become aware that new forms of behaviour have to be adopted if the culture is to change and that certain interpersonal skills will be required to support this behaviour.

Depending on the circumstances and the extent of previous discussions between the senior managers, the goals stage can take between two and six days. It usually begins with a two-day workshop, followed by a few half-day sessions.

Critical Success Factors (CSFs)

Having clarified the goals, the senior management team will need to spend more time in developing clear measures of success to monitor the improvement process. Several strategic decisions will have to be taken before these measures can be arrived at. They tend to cover four main areas:

1. The customer: how do your customers see you?
2. Financial: how do your shareholders see you?
3. Internal business perspective: what must you excel at?
4. Improvement (particularly personal): how do you continue to get better?

It would be too sweeping to say that there is no point in introducing a culture change if it does not produce tangible benefits. However, too many organizations spend years doing what appears to be all the right things but achieving little. This usually happens because appropriate critical success factors and short-term goals were not agreed at the outset.

The importance of this stage must also be emphasized. One benefit of discussing CSFs thoroughly is that it provides a further opportunity to explore and clarify the strategic vision. Another is that everyone understands and 'owns' the measures that are eventually agreed. This activity is a natural continuation of the goal clarification stage.

Self-assessment

In most organizations that achieve successful change, the critical success factors act as a backdrop for a careful review of the existing business. You will already have identified any significant changes that are necessary to allow the new culture to flourish, which will probably encompass the following areas:

- customer orientation;
- administrative systems and organization structure;
- people systems (reward, recognition, appraisal, and so on);
- leadership;
- innovation.

You will find that there are some organizational barriers to change. Most organizations are structured according to functions, whereas most business processes, such as invoicing or developing a customer relationship, require input from several functions across the business. Were your cost centres set up to reflect a customer need or a financial one?

After you have identified the changes and barriers, you need to decide how to address them. The changes that even the best businesses need to make are often substantial. Changes that are recommended by external consultants stand little chance of being achieved because of the lack of ownership for them internally.

Most organizations that do achieve change use a team of people from within the business to make the assessments and present recommendations, although they may be supported by 'process skills' consultants. This has the following advantages:

- the recommendations are owned within the organization;
- the new culture can be practised with the team;
- the level of understanding of the change can be raised throughout the company;
- the senior managers can get some experience of practising the new culture.

Usually a steering group will agree their preferences for immediate action, and define the support needed and their role in providing this. Working with two or three teams, a skilled facilitator would help to prepare sound recommendations for actions on the priority areas. These teams can usually be expected to meet for about two hours per week and for about 12 weeks.

Cascade the aims

The senior management team often spends a great deal of time, quite rightly, getting to grips with the fundamentals of the new culture and deciding how to energize the organization. They then make the mistake of cascading the message down to middle managers and supervisors, and then to non-managerial employees without giving sufficient thought to the consequences.

Non-managerial employees usually become excited by the vision. Strategic change, as opposed to thinly disguised cost cutting and job losses, will create a better workplace. Usually employees will find that they are listened to more, trusted more, and given more responsibility if they want it. They then look to their supervisors to help and support them, in the way that they have been led to expect, and nothing happens: end of excitement; beginning of disillusionment.

This problem usually occurs because the supervisor, who has perhaps the greatest behavioural change to make, has not had sufficient input into the process to have ownership of it. Neither have they been given the technical or interpersonal skills to support the change. Therefore, following on and developing from the senior management team's induction, the middle managers must be helped to understand the vision. They need as much, if not more, training as the senior managers.

If the process of communicating the vision is conducted by outsiders alone, this can indicate to employees a lack of commitment on the part of senior managers. In some organizations consultants may begin the 'cascade' process, but the aim should always be for the staff to identify how they want the communication process to continue.

If middle managers are as excited by the change as senior managers, this will result in a change in their behaviour. As people are much more aware of what their managers do than what they say, this change will be noticeable. The cascade process can then be continued to involve front-line employees with the proper support from middle managers.

Develop skills

The steering group needs to establish some priorities for developing people's skills, which will probably involve some of the following areas:

- management skills (known as process skills), which include individual behaviour; coaching and counselling; team behaviour;
- technical skills, particularly for employees, such as problem solving and knowledge of industry best practice;
- interpersonal skills, particularly for employees, including teamwork; customer care; and organizational influencing.

In organizations where the change process has gone through most smoothly, the initial emphasis has always been on management skills and the first managers to undergo development have been the steering group.

Support the teams

One cornerstone of modern organizational cultures is that people should naturally work in teams. One decision for the steering group will be the extent and speed with which you want to introduce them. Even if you believe that your organization already works this way, it is worthwhile exploring the extent to which they are really being employed and the opportunities to do so more widely.

Over the last two decades we have seen an emergence of teams as a unit of organizational structure from their embryonic beginnings as quality circles and similar groups. There are still today organizations that claim to have teams in place yet where the individuals work alone and have little constructive dialogue with one another. Their talents, creativity and commitment are being wasted and morale inevitably declines.

Shifts in culture take a long time. Steady improvement is achieved not by one quick stride but by a number of small steps. Every success reinforces the process of change and gives it momentum while also boosting the confidence of the teams.

Counselling

Once front-line employees have been given a clear picture of the new culture and the skills to make it happen, then real improvement starts to take place, often with stunning rapidity. Some middle managers, however, may feel trapped, no longer able to carry out their traditional role of monitoring and not yet comfortable with the role that they do have of supporting and coaching.

In many traditional businesses, counselling is seen as a 'soft' activity. Yet those businesses which succeed invariably provide some form of confidential support for their managers. A good example is British Telecom, which committed an entire department to providing management counselling.

Ongoing review

Organizations often set up a steering group to focus efforts on the change process. The purpose of the group, its composition, how often it meets, and how it communicates with the rest of the company need to be agreed.

Most companies use the steering group as an opportunity for the management team to try out different ways of meeting and working and to learn new skills.

Targeted marketing

Throughout the change process you will need to develop plans for a targeted approach to marketing the new culture. This will begin within the organization but will eventually include external marketing. Initially the intention is to create a demand for the new culture and later to explain the process in detail.

The external phase, which often doesn't start until 6 to 18

months into the process of change, will involve suppliers and then customers. Members of the steering group will probably establish the marketing strategy for the culture change process, identify the resources necessary and allocate appropriate budgets. They will monitor its effectiveness and regularly review the approach adopted. Clearly, it is important for marketing to be carried out in a professional manner and so planning usually begins at the steering group meeting about three or four months into the change process.

NOTES

1   Blanchard, K, Zigarmi, P and Zigarmi, D (1986) *Leadership and the One Minute Manager*, Collins, London

2   Guest, R H, Hersey, P and Blanchard, K H (1986) *Organizational Change Through Effective Leadership*, Prentice-Hall, London

3   Hersey, P and Blanchard, K H (1988) *Management of Organizational Behaviour*, Prentice-Hall, London

4   Wilson, G (1993) *Making Change Happen*, FT Pitman, London

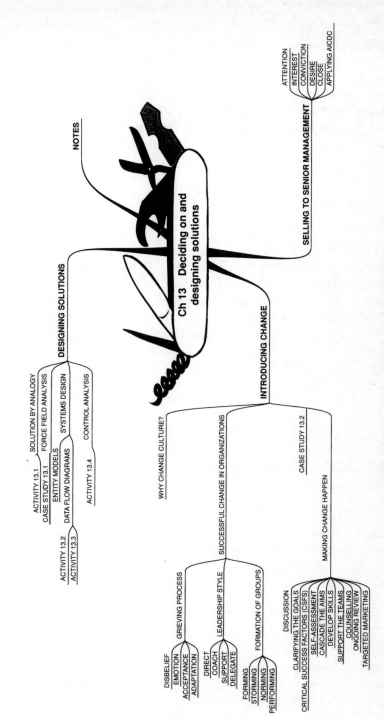

Figure 13.6 *Overview of Chapter 13*

CHAPTER 14

Effect and evaluate

This book has discussed the skills, the tools and techniques that are needed and the individual strengths that are necessary for effective problem solving. This short final chapter will highlight the importance of the last stage in the PRIDE model – effect and evaluate.

Groups often take a problem to the point of developing a solution and then leave others to put it into effect, or at least cease to meet formally once the solution is in place. In my experience it is better for the team members to devise and implement the solution in many cases. This allows them to revise it and also ensures that the original difficulty is fully resolved. They will use the plan that they have developed and monitor for themselves any changes that are necessary, obviously making sure that they do so in a structured and safe manner.

All team-based problem solving has two agendas. The first is to achieve the team members' objectives for the task. These may have been set for them, or by them, and relate to the problem that they were trying to solve. The second agenda is to improve the team members' powers of analysis and teamwork. Before they disperse, or go on to tackle another problem, it is important that both of these agendas are properly addressed.

CONTROLS

The previous chapter looked at controls and how they should be designed in to the solution. No solution is complete if it doesn't somehow monitor the results, even if the cause has been completely eradicated.

Passive

Monitoring should be passive in the sense that problems should be visible and not require active detection.

Analysis

The monitors should require the minimum of analysis. Any analysis, which includes even simple calculations, can introduce more problems and create delays. Feedback is always better if it is immediate even if you decide not to react immediately.

Charts

Using simple graphics or coloured lights built in to a system can make the detection of further problems easy. One group created a simple system of coloured yellow disks on the floor. If the disks could be seen then it meant that they weren't covered. If they weren't covered then a cylinder of a particular chemical was missing from the production floor. If it was missing, then by the time it could be fetched it would not reach ambient temperature before it was used and it was the variable temperature of this chemical that affected most of the variation in quality of the product.

CASE STUDY 14.1

Nowadays, with sophisticated computer systems controlling many aspects of our lives, with common components and many features of electronic systems unused, it is always worth the team exploring whether something else in their solution can be used to flag problems. For example, the circuitry used to produce a certain piece of hospital equipment includes a 'chip' that processes information about the vital signs of a patient. The chip is actually the same as one used in aircraft systems. In the hospital, the system merely displayed the information on a screen for nurses to make a visual assessment as they passed. In the aircraft another part of the chip transmitted warning information to a remote display in the cockpit if the electronics appeared to be malfunctioning. By adapting the hospital equipment to make use of this part of the chip it was possible to provide a remote display at the nurses station to indicate immediately when a patient had inadvertently dislodged a sensor.

The concept of failsafe design that originated in Japan actively prevents problems by making them impossible to happen in the first place. One car manufacturer is said to have spent a weekend producing four-door hatchback cars because one side of the production line was fitting two-door variant panels and the other side was fitting one-door variants. Although there was a lot more to this problem than simple assembly, had the one and two door panels used a different alignment of fittings the whole problem would have been avoided.

OBJECTIVES

The task

The team's solution should have met the goals set for it. So part of the assessment should focus on these.

The people

While a final process review gives members an opportunity to explore how they felt being part of the team, it is also useful to allow people a few moments to reflect on and share their personal learning from being involved. This is especially useful where their own personal development plan calls for evidence of prior learning as many competency-based approaches do.

Necessary and sufficient

Whether it is in their assessment of their effectiveness or of the effect of their solution, groups are often too hard on themselves. It is important that the result is sufficient and that the effort put in was necessary. But they shouldn't seek a perfect fix and shouldn't monitor their effort only in terms of the solution they produced.

Pay back?

There is a simple model used in training to assess its effectiveness which may also be applied in other situations. In a problem-solving context, the four steps might be:

1. To what extent has the original problem been resolved?
2. To what extent have future recurrences been prevented?
3. Have other opportunities to apply the same solution to other problems been sufficiently explored?
4. How will other people, later, find out about and apply the same solution to new situations?

With these in mind the real impact of the team and its work can be assessed.

PROCESS REVIEW

The general approach to process reviews is explained earlier. For the final review, however, it is useful to structure the discussion after a more general sharing has happened – this is because the people may never meet formally again and so there is limited time for thoughts to emerge.

What went well

It is worth agreeing what the members of the group felt went well. They will probably try to add some of the negatives too and these can be helpful but need to be kept in perspective.

Transferable skills

Then look at the skills that they have acquired and how they will take them forward with them to new jobs, roles and experiences.

Appreciate/wish

Share feelings about each other: 'I really appreciated how you could rally us together when we were floundering. I wish you would recognize that strength and be prepared to use it more often.'

Learning from the group

Finally, share the things that have been learned about working together.

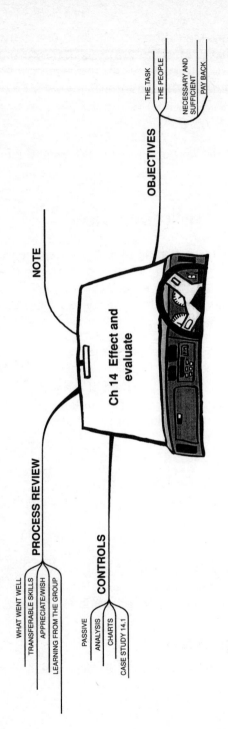

Figure 14.1 *Overview of Chapter 14*

Index

Visit Kogan Page on-line

Comprehensive information on
Kogan Page titles

Features include

- complete catalogue listings,
  including book reviews and
  descriptions

- on-line discounts on a variety
  of titles

- special monthly promotions

- information and discounts on
  NEW titles and BESTSELLING titles

- a secure shopping basket facility
  for on-line ordering

- infoZones, with links and
  information on specific areas of
  interest

PLUS everything you need to know
about KOGAN PAGE

http://www.kogan-page.co.uk